BattersbyHowat

Architectural Signatures Canada

BattersbyHowat

Tuns Press

Tuns Press
Faculty of Architecture and Planning
Dalhousie University
Halifax, Nova Scotia, Canada
tunspress.dal.ca

Tuns Press Editorial Board
Christine Macy, Dean
Essy Baniassad
Sarah Bonnemaison
Brian Carter
Frank Palermo
Michelangelo Sabatino
Donald Westin, Press Manager

BattersbyHowat
Editor: Brian Carter
Designed by Chris Allen with Marion Lacoste, Burnkit.
Printed by Friesens

© 2013 by Tuns Press
All Rights Reserved. Published in May 2013
Printed in Canada

Library and Archives Canada Cataloguing in Publication

Battersby Howat / Brian Carter, ed.

(Architectural Signatures Canada)
ISBN 978-0-929112-58-9

1. Battersby, David. 2. Howat, Heather. 3. Architecture–
British Columbia–History–20th century. 4. Architecture–
British Columbia–History–21st century. I. Carter, Brian,
1942 - II. Series: Architectural Signatures Canada.

NA749.B387B382012   720.92'271   C2012-906423-8

Contents

Preface Christine Macy — 6
Introduction Brian Carter — 9
Domestic Topographies Christopher Macdonald — 10
Selected Works — 14
Postscript Brian Carter — 85

Gulf Island — 14
North Bend — 22
Bonetti — 28
2386 Cornwall — 34
Gambier 1 — 40
Tolmie — 52
Whistler — 60
Salt Spring Island — 66
Gambier 2 — 72
Fairmile — 80

Introduction

Brian Carter

"Soon you realize that there's a difference between the world you're living in and the world you want to live in. The world you want to live in is a human world, not an objective one; it's not an environment but a home; it's not the world you see but the world you build out of what you see…the important categories are what you have to do and what you want to do — in other words, necessity and freedom."

The Educated Imagination, Northrop Frye, p.19–20. Indiana University Press, 1964.

Heather Howat and David Battersby, like many architects, are frequently preoccupied by what they have to do and what they want to do. However, in the time that they have been working together, these two young architects have rigorously explored the very different territories of necessity and freedom.

Their explorations have been focused by a commitment to an integrative approach to design. For BattersbyHowat, this is an approach that entails looking beyond the confines of architecture. It examines the nature of the land and the vegetation that it supports. It considers the form and thoughtful siting of buildings and the construction of both external and internal spaces. It is an approach that is inspired by what they see. It is an approach that, albeit especially relevant at a time when resources are limited, is difficult to detect in much of the contemporary architecture in North America.

For these two designers this approach is deeply rooted. With degrees in landscape architecture and interior design from the University of Manitoba, David Battersby and Heather Howat went on to study architecture at Dalhousie University before establishing their practice in Vancouver in 1996. And, while the siting of buildings and the outdoor spaces that they have designed clearly demonstrate preoccupations with landscape, their thoughtful selection of materials, detailing, and the consideration of assemblies that define spaces within these buildings also signal other levels of integration and precision.

The work of BattersbyHowat, perhaps inevitably for an emerging practice, is made up of modest projects. It has included the renewal of buildings to create spaces to work and places to relax. However it has been primarily focused on the design of houses. Working closely alongside clients with differing needs and who seek to live in different places has prompted David Battersby and Heather Howat to look carefully at landscapes and enclosed space. Consequently the designs of these houses have clearly been inspired by settings that range from confined sites in the Vancouver area to remote islands off the coast of British Columbia. Each of the designs outlined in this book, then, clearly references necessity and freedom.

Domestic Topographies

Christopher Macdonald

In both the emergence and ensuing development of a modern architectural idiom in Canada's Pacific Northwest, designs for the detached family home have served an important role as crucibles of exploration and research. New materials and building technologies have been allied with challenges to conventional social habit, while the rugged terrain, lush vegetation, and benign climate have provided a profound measure to the artifice of design. The domestic projects of BattersbyHowat fully embrace this tradition and bear witness to the potential of 'patient searching' to discover experiences of uncommon poise. With over 16 years of practiced accomplishment, David Battersby and Heather Howat are consistently producing compositions possessing at once clarity and suggestive potential—what might be thought of as domestic topographies.

The affinity between the domestic environments illustrated here and the landscapes that they inhabit is remarkable. This is true not only when the spatial logics of the houses echo the geography of often rugged, wild sites but also prevail when the surroundings are largely construed by the designers themselves. This ability to connect the most general position of the houses with their broad landscape context while cultivating a much more local, qualified exterior world provides a consistent theme to the work. Without question, this thoughtful consideration enriches the quality of experience both inside and out. Surrounding local landscapes are often portrayed as distinct ancillary 'rooms' rather than the direct extrusion of interior configurations and surfaces. At times these spaces claim their status as gardens, but always expand upon the uneasy resolve between building and landscape so often evident in contemporary practice.

While a taut modern screen of expansive glazing may provide literal separation, passage from interior to the landscape is characterized by a sense of deep threshold — a quality shared with many of the interior transitions as well. The orchestrated approach and attenuated arrival offer the most obvious instance of this quality — present in virtually all of the designs included here — yet the cultivation of dimensionally generous overlaps between interior spaces occurs more generally — a deliberate tactic resisting the 'thin' inclinations of frame construction. Most explicitly, the deployment of finely wrought custom cabinets serve this role, while in their scale and finesse providing a kind of bridge between the clear organizational order of the house and the realm of furnishings and other accoutrements of human habitation which will follow construction.

The tartan motif to these planning strategies — where the thickness of a cupboard serves as a de facto wall thickness — also promotes the emergence of incidental spaces that provide counterpoint and emphasis to the more functionally deliberate spaces in the houses. Against the aggregated private spaces of beds and baths and the more nuanced contours of common living areas, there exists a kind of grown-up version of the child's house-under-a-table experience. The intimacy of these exceptional moments provides a memorable occasion through which a house might be rendered your own — perhaps fulfilling in architectural terms the role of garden within the expanse of a natural setting.

Finally, it remains to speak to the sheer care and attention to execution that is so evident throughout the BattersbyHowat portfolio — the extent to which all decisions at all scales and purposes are so considered. In this respect, the practice situates its design ethos securely in a modern project that is comprehensive and complete, inheriting the special responsibilities that such a history demands. While at first blush there is unquestionably a level of consistency to both material and spatial palettes, it is in fact the discovery of difference and distinctions from project to project that speaks to the confidence and maturity of the work — and to the systematic enquiry that underpins its successes. Each house possesses degrees of drama alongside degrees of solitary stasis and the expressive pleasures of a matchbooked veneer are almost certainly lodged within the cool calmness of a well-rehearsed modernist background.

Collectively, the work suggests the capacity to engage more varied and more public purposes, with the consequence of becoming considerably more accessible. If it is a virtue of single-family house designs to provide highly focused explorations of a very particular nature, this is balanced by the inherent inability for the houses to be directly experienced by a broad audience. In offering eloquent testimony to the work, this current volume invites a larger public to imaginatively inhabit the projects — to enjoy this timely evocation of the firm, commodious, and delightful work of BattersbyHowat.

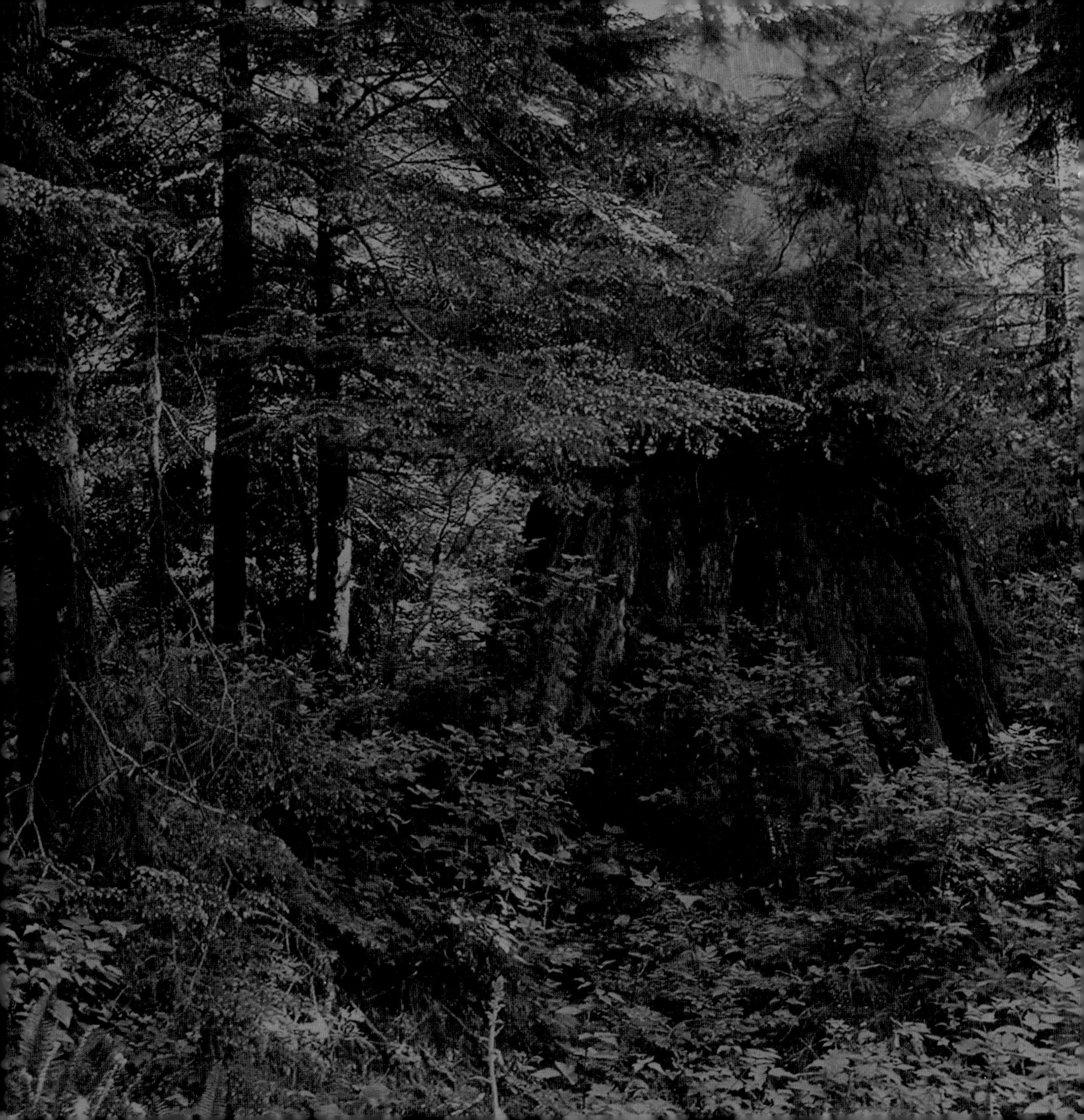

Selected Works

Gulf Island

Building Area
2500 ft² (230 m²)

Location
Gulf Islands, British Columbia

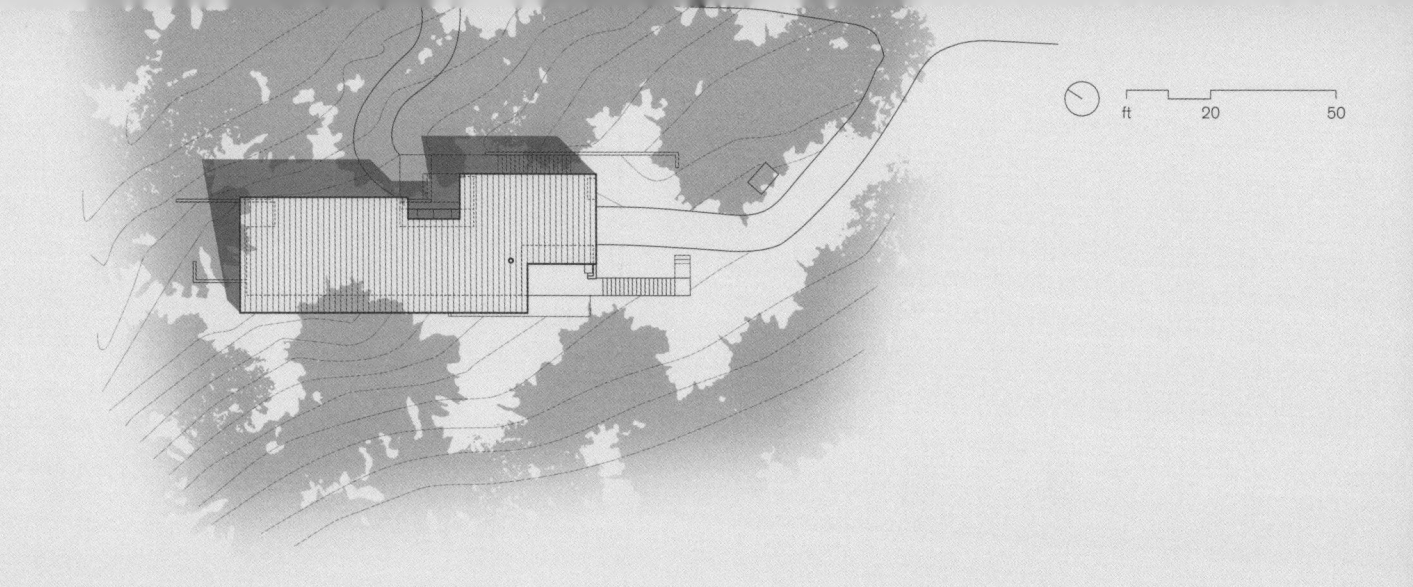

Building Type
Single-family residence

Year
2004

The house is located in the Southern Gulf Islands on the site of a former cottage. To the north and east the site is defined by public roads. New construction has been set back from the original structure and located on a strip of land to the west where there are views out over a secluded bay. This avoided the need to remove any trees, and at the same time made it possible to create a new entry for the house while retaining existing points of access onto the site for pedestrians and vehicles.

The foundation and lower level of the house are concrete and stucco. These materials anchor the house to its surroundings and create a base for lighter construction above. This includes a zinc roof that folds onto the north elevation to form both a wall and a canopy. Wood framing is exploited at both roof and floor levels and it cantilevers out on the south facing elevation to provide shading and underline the formal qualities of the house. Prefabricated roof trusses, designed with extensions of the top and bottom chords, articulate the prosaic assembly. The bottom chord has been extended so as to express the cubic nature of the interior volume and at the same time inscribe an obvious datum against which to read the varied topography of the site. The depth of the roof truss is revealed as a recessed mass between the elongated interior volume and its zinc clad wrapper.

The entrance to the house is situated within a gap on the northern elevation. This gap is also referenced in section by slippages in the roof planes and the points where the stair creates an opening in the floors. External walls are protected with a rain-screen cladding of horizontal slats of yellow cedar to define areas of human habitation, entrances, decks and patios.

Exploded Axo

Zinc roofing and upper chord of truss

Volume of truss web

Interior volume defined by framed elements including the bottom chord of truss

Concrete foundation and stucco clay perimeter walls which delineate the footprint of pre-existing cabin

17

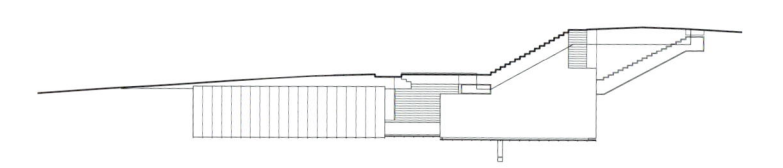

North Elevation

Main Floor

1 Entry
2 Powder Room
3 Den
4 Living / Dining
5 Kitchen
6 Laundry
7 Master Bathroom
8 Master Bedroom
9 Dressing Hall

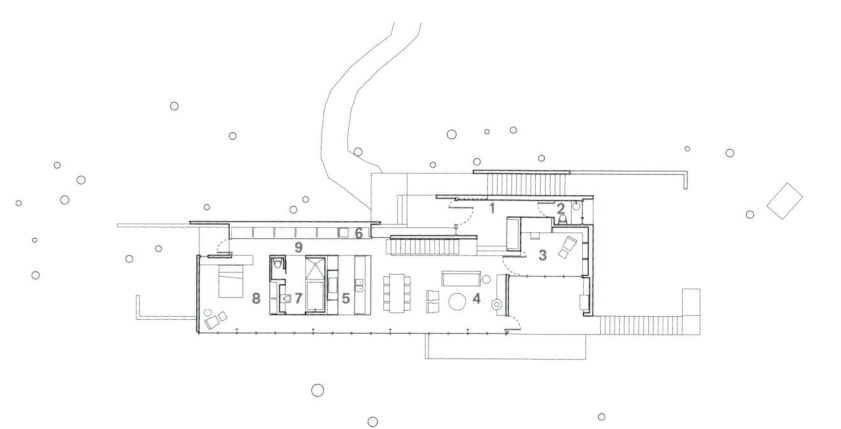

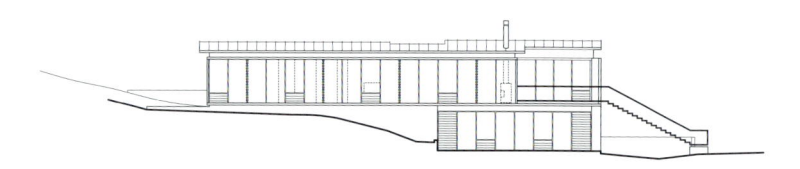

South Elevation

ft 20 50

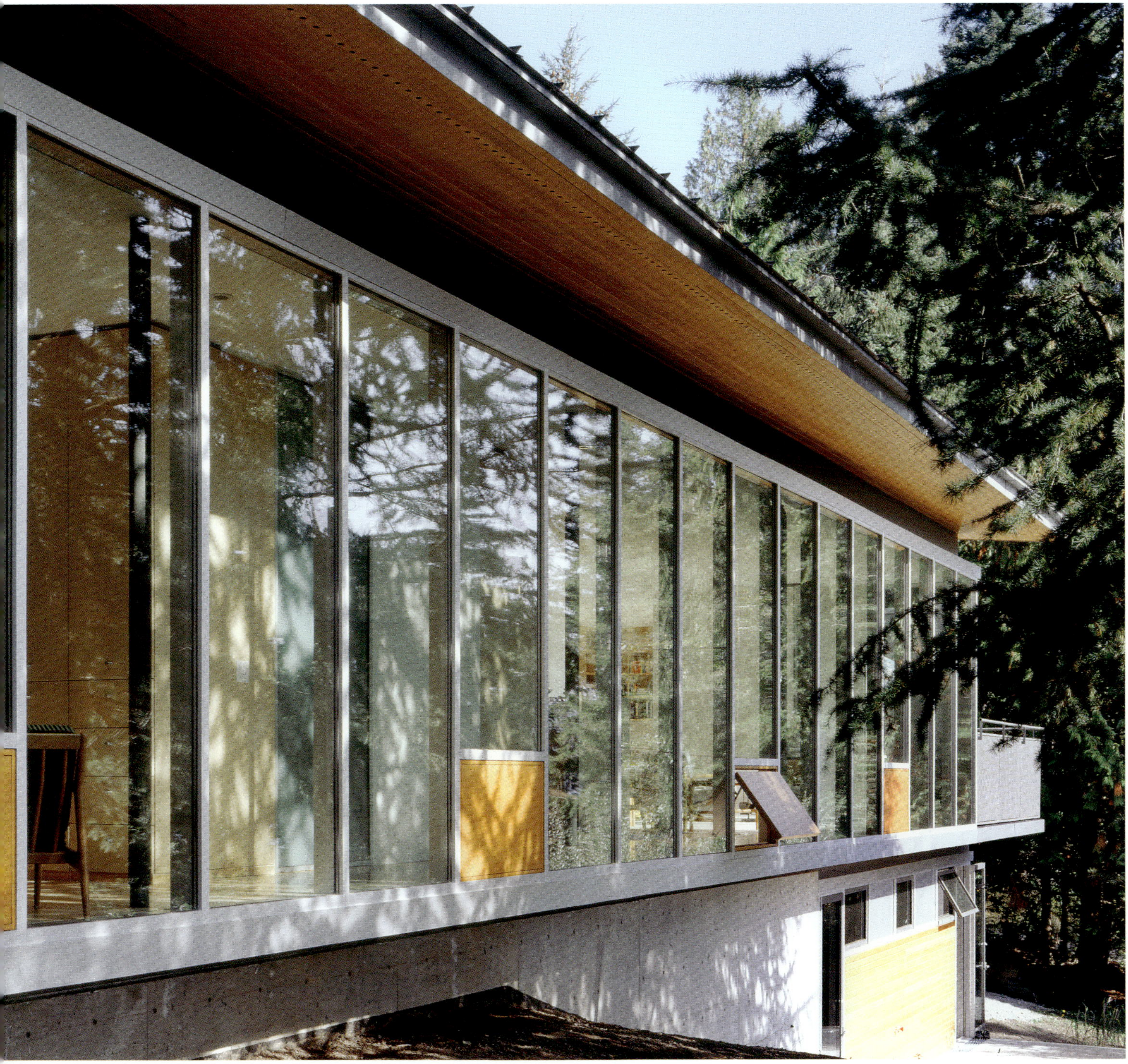

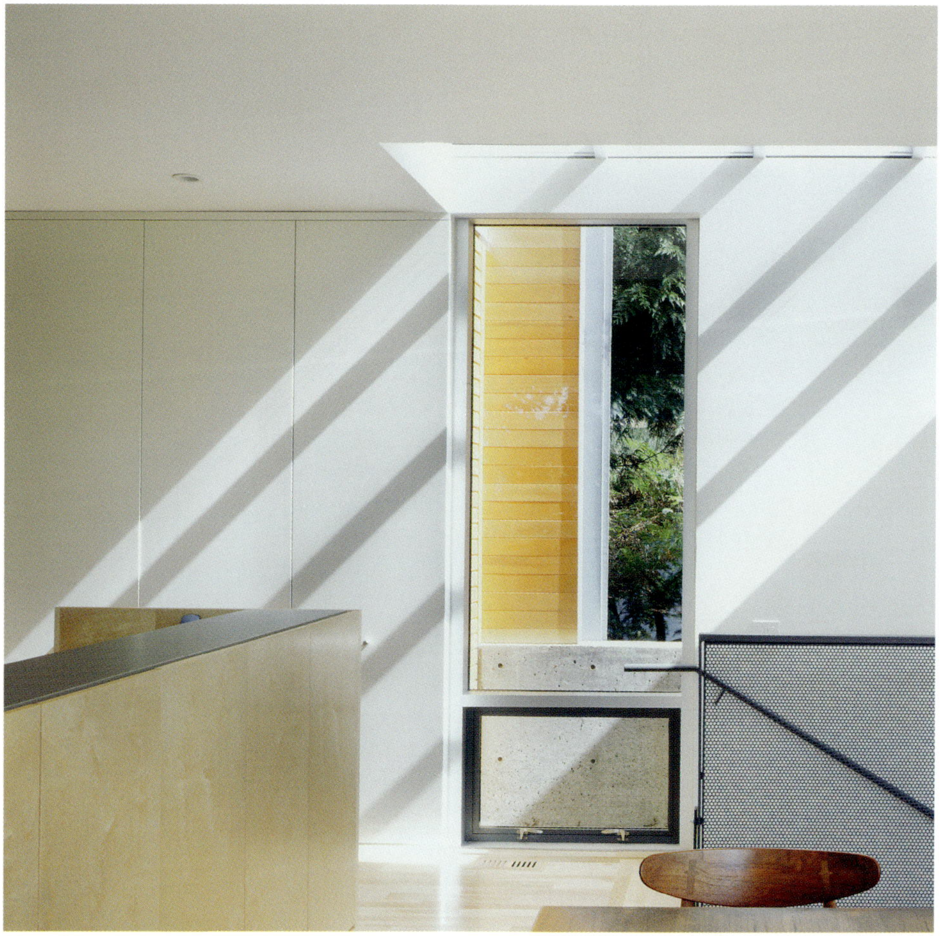

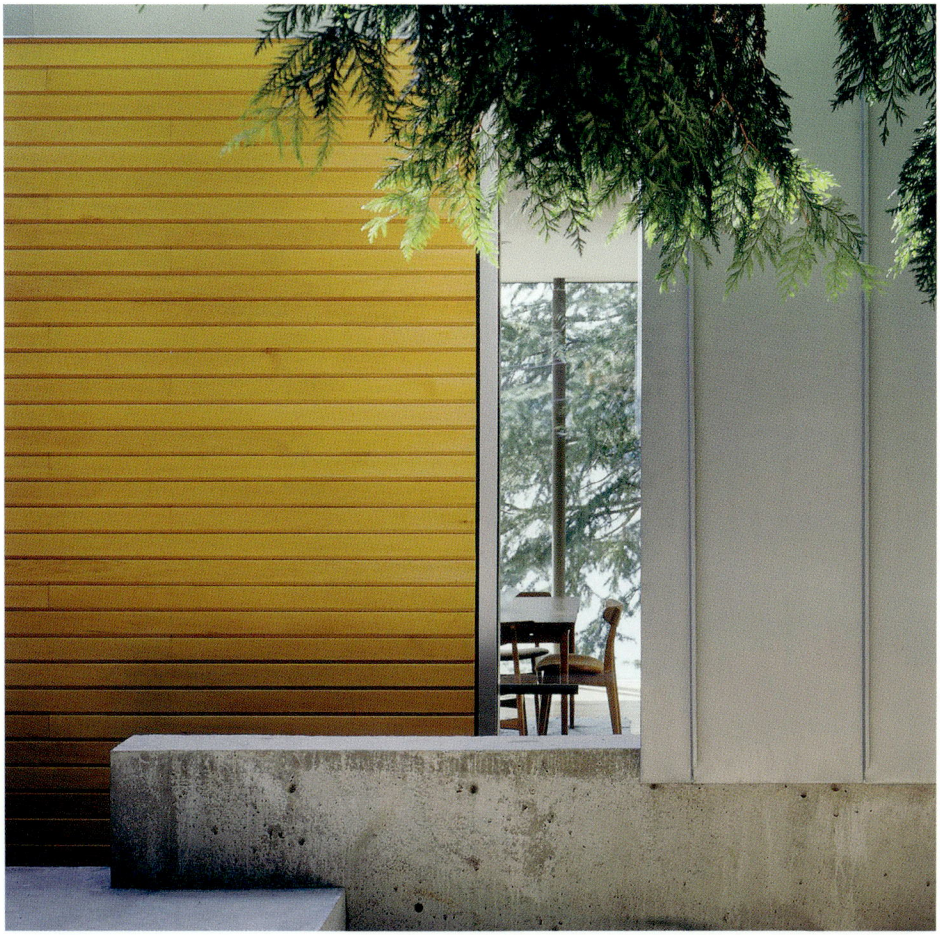

North Bend

This site in the Pacific Northwest is covered with ferns, vine maples, and second-growth hemlock and fir while also containing charred old-growth stumps that recall former landscapes. The proposed house was sited so that these oversized relics, and the delicate flora growing from them, would be positioned alongside newly created domestic living spaces. Conceived as a long, narrow box clad in dark-stained siding, the shadowy architectural form has been designed to recede visually and give prominence to the landscape and natural topography of the site. In strategic locations, this siding has been extended to create screens that would filter light and provide privacy during the day while transforming into lit filtered planes indicating occupation at night. The timber cladding will contrast with the board-formed concrete of the foundation from which much of the house structure is to be cantilevered. A 'thickened' wall, expressed in plan through an intentional dispersal of millwork at the perimeter, will be modulated by a series of cut-out volumes lined in yellow cedar. Irregular window widths and operable yellow cedar panels within these recesses will create a visual rhythm sympathetic to the surrounding forest.

Building Area
5000 ft² (465 m²)

Location
North Bend, Washington, USA

Building Type
Single-family residence

Unbuilt

Main Floor

1. Entry
2. Kitchen
3. Living / Dining
4. Outdoor Terrace
5. Guest Bathroom
6. Guest Bedroom
7. Exercise Room
8. Outdoor Deck
9. Office
10. Powder Room
11. Rainwater Collector
12. Driveway

Upper Floor

1. Master Bedroom
2. Dressing Area
3. Master Bathroom
4. Laundry Room
5. Bridge
6. Bathroom
7. Bedroom
8. Family Room
9. Upper Level Courtyard

ft 10 20

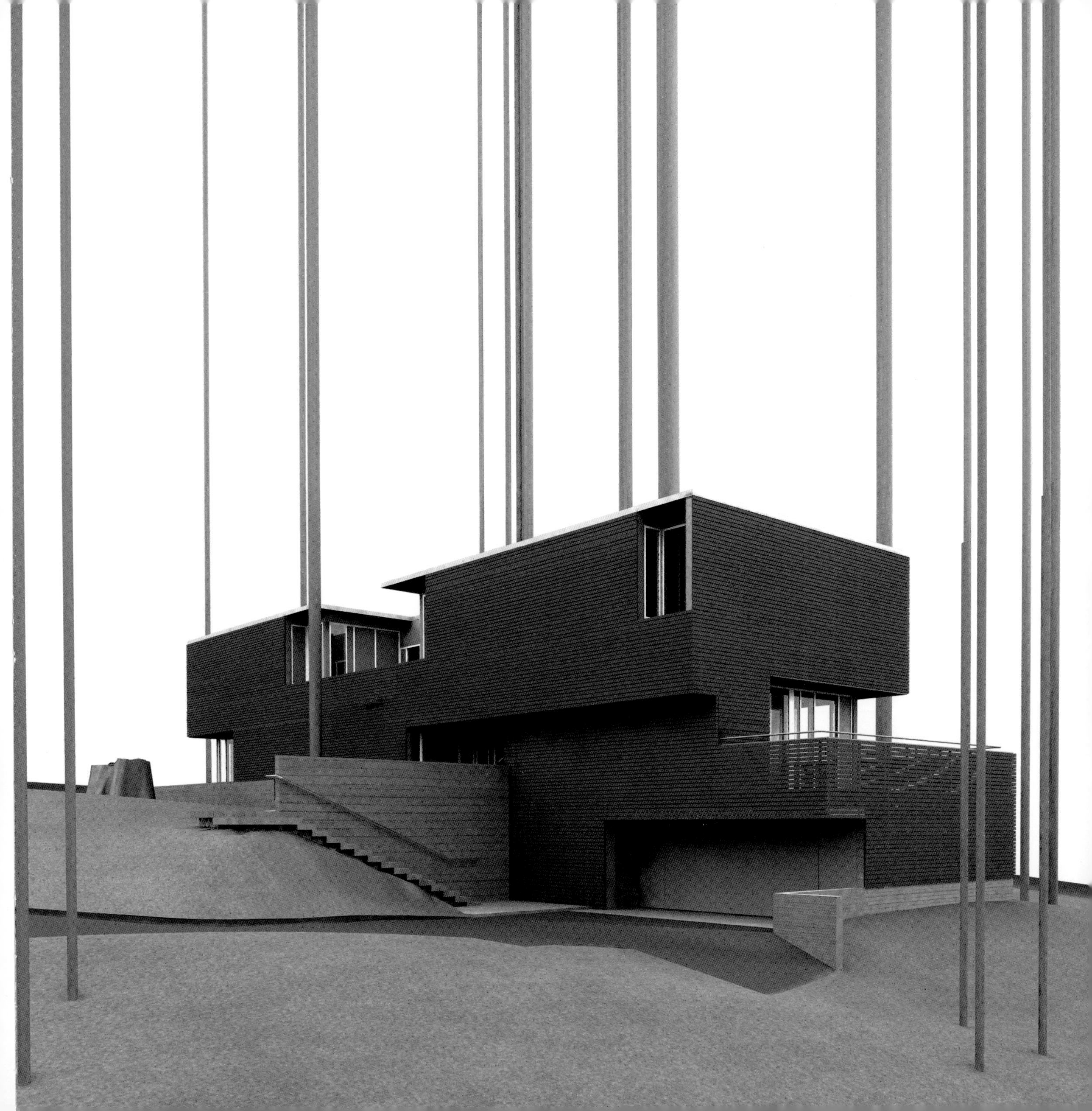

Bonetti

Located on an oddly shaped wooded lot in West Vancouver, this house is approached by a meandering drive that traverses a seasonal creek. A heavily-treed hillside defines the northern property boundary, while the forest thins down a slope toward a railway line. A neighbouring house is visible to the east.

The design for this house is based on an L-shaped courtyard plan. The public side of the house—an enigmatic stucco shell that faces the street—shields an articulated inner courtyard lined with wooden slats. This space is configured to accommodate outdoor entertaining and family activities. It offers a panoramic overview of the site and additional glimpses of the landscape beyond while maintaining privacy. Horizontal glazing over the kitchen counter, for instance, connects immediately to the landscape of lush ferns and rocks against which the house is embedded.

The potential sprawl and warren-like nature of a large single-family house is addressed by connecting the modulated interior spaces, with a large double height volume that cuts a swath through the house.

Building Area
5500 ft² (510 m²)

Location
West Vancouver, British Columbia

Building Type
Single-family residence

Year
2005

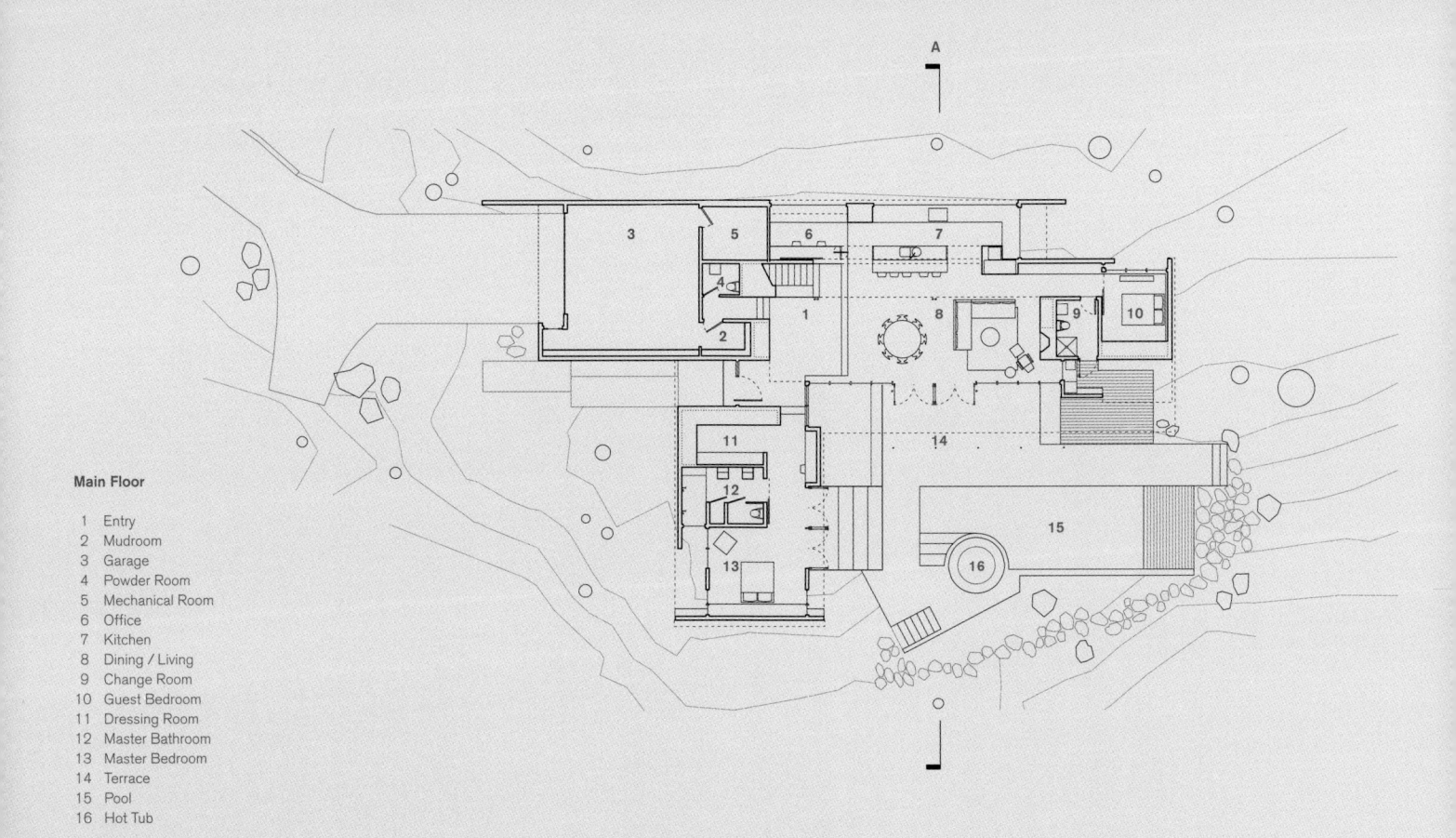

Main Floor

1. Entry
2. Mudroom
3. Garage
4. Powder Room
5. Mechanical Room
6. Office
7. Kitchen
8. Dining / Living
9. Change Room
10. Guest Bedroom
11. Dressing Room
12. Master Bathroom
13. Master Bedroom
14. Terrace
15. Pool
16. Hot Tub

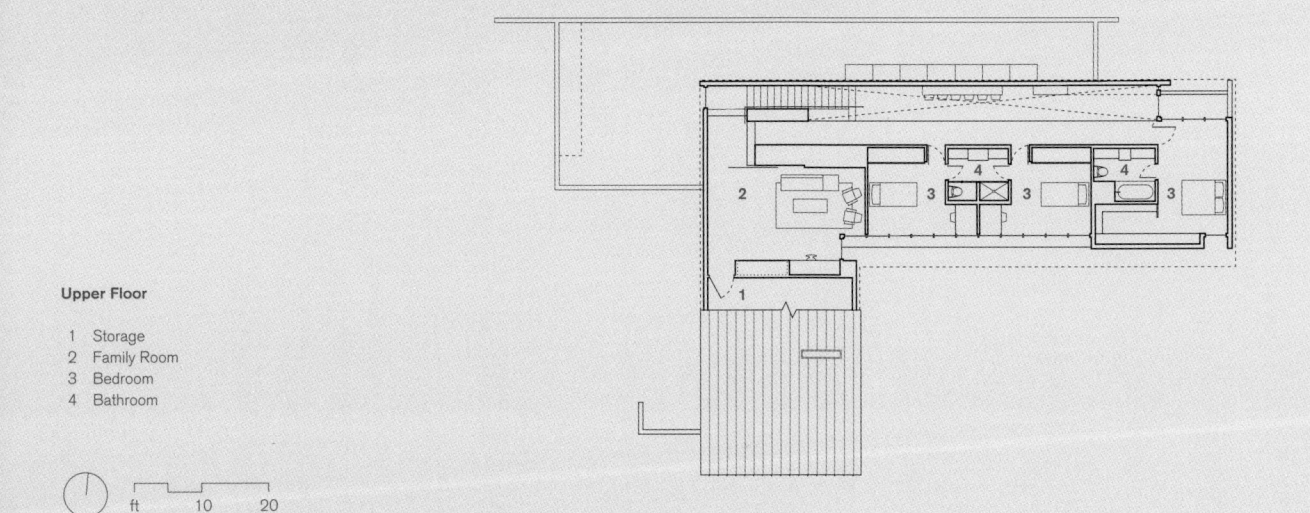

Upper Floor

1. Storage
2. Family Room
3. Bedroom
4. Bathroom

Section A

1. Shower
2. Hall
3. Living / Dining
4. Kitchen
5. Terrace
6. Pool

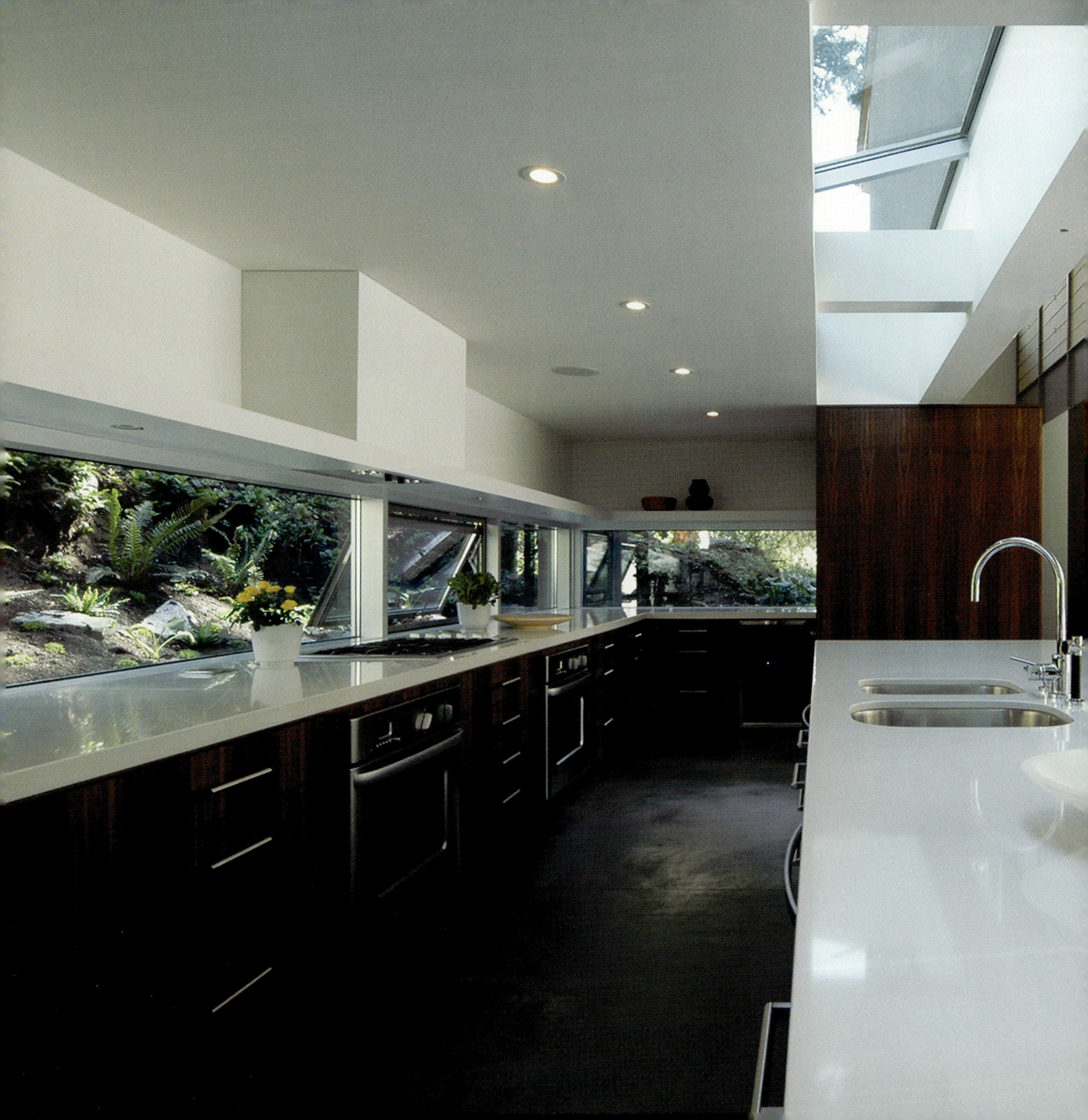

33

2386 Cornwall

Building Area
7830 sq. ft² (727 m²)

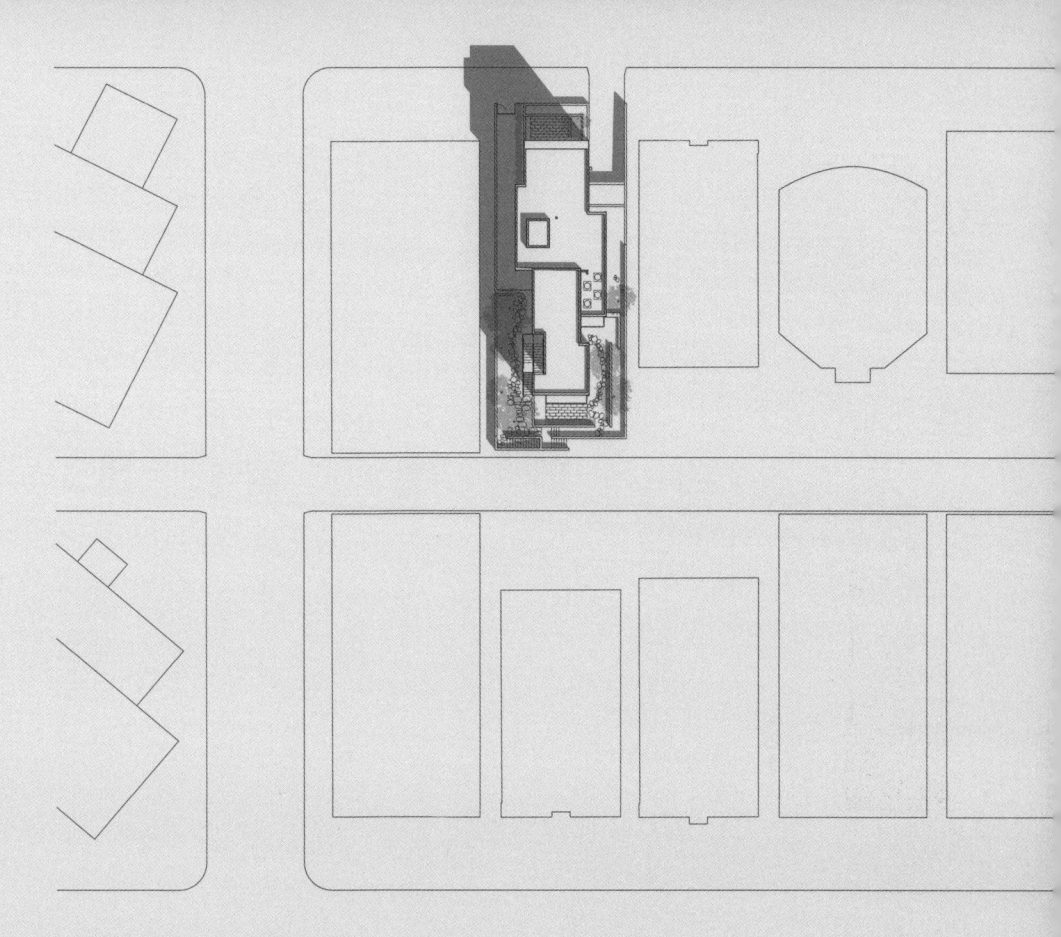

Location
Kitsilano, Vancouver, British Columbia

Building Type
Multi-family residential

Year
2007

A speculative development prominently located opposite Kitsilano Beach in Vancouver, this multi-family building contains four residential units. Each suite occupies an entire floor. The long, narrow mid-block site has a north-orientated view towards the ocean and Stanley Park peninsula, but is overlooked by adjacent properties to the east and west. Consequently, the project has been planned around a series of staggered north-south concrete walls so as to articulate interior and exterior spaces while maintaining privacy for the new residents and their neighbours. The resultant exterior spaces between the new and adjacent structures form a series of landscaped courts that serve as an amenity for the inhabitants of both the new and existing buildings.

This strategy also influences the internal planning of the units, where floors, walls, and ceilings have been built in concrete. These elements have been combined with black walnut cabinetry. Subtle lateral shifts and level changes disguise the spatial boundaries of the dwellings, while the open ends of the building — in-filled with glazing, perforated metal panels, and red cedar siding — admit light and reveal views.

1 Site Condition

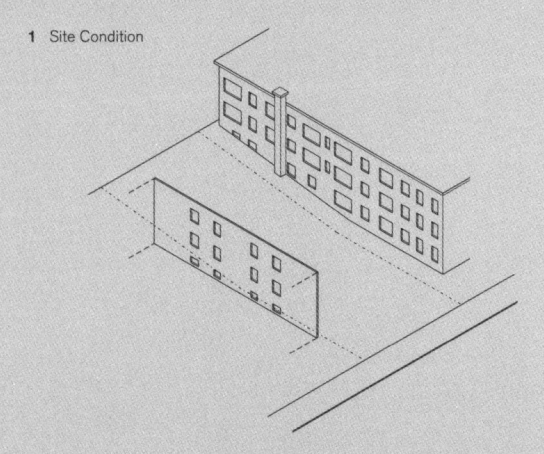

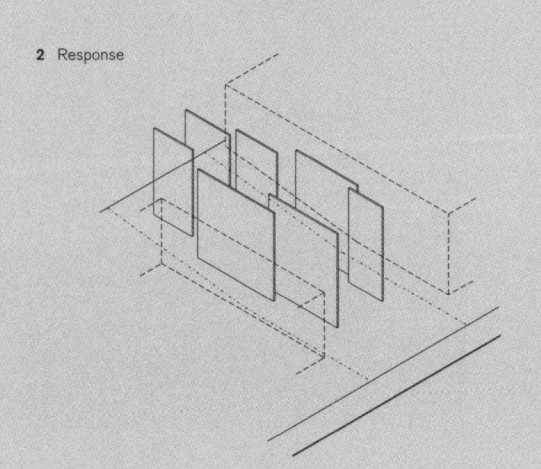

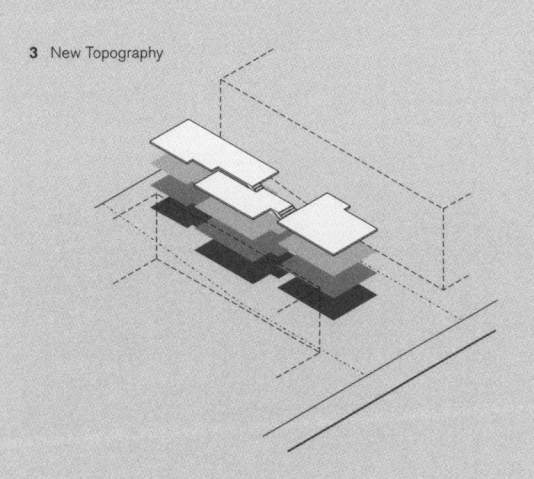

2 Response

3 New Topography

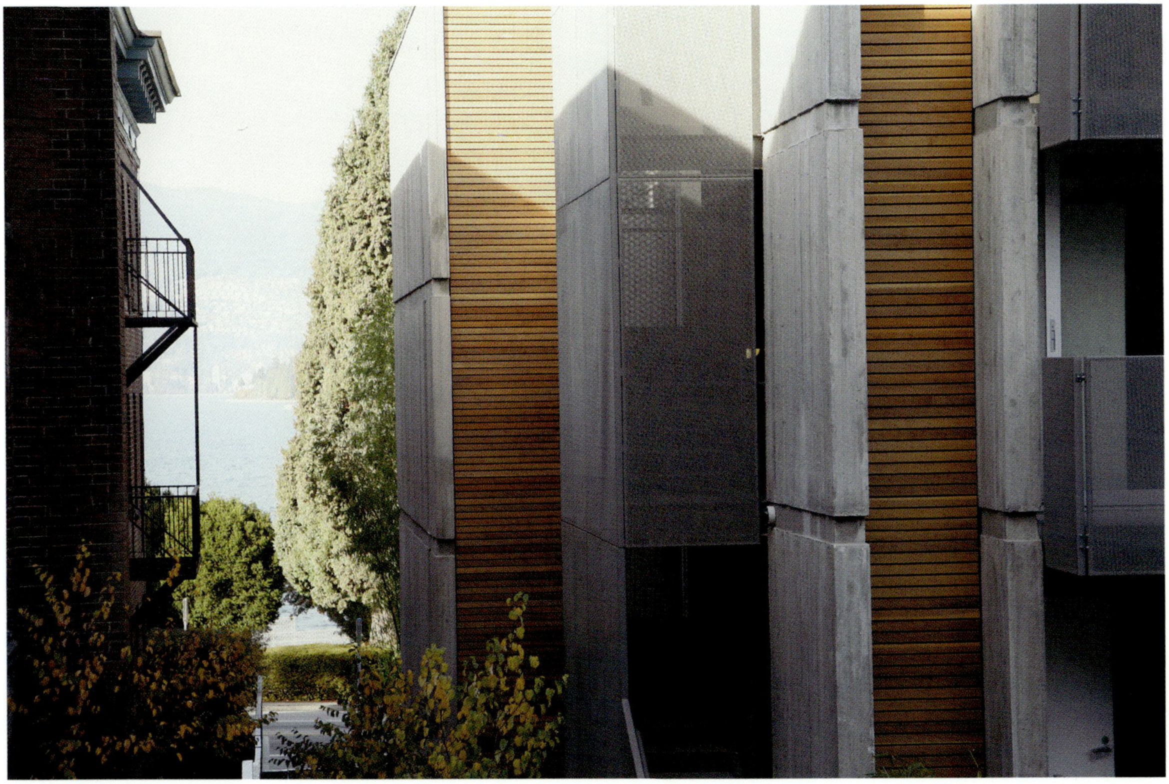

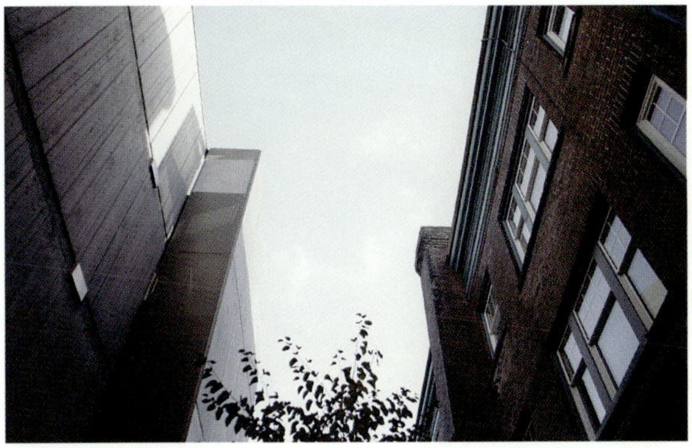

Ground Floor

1. Outdoor Terrace
2. Living Room
3. Dining
4. Kitchen
5. Guest Bathroom
6. Guest Bedroom
7. Powder Room
8. Master Bathroom
9. Master Bedroom
10. Elevator
11. Entry
12. Courtyard

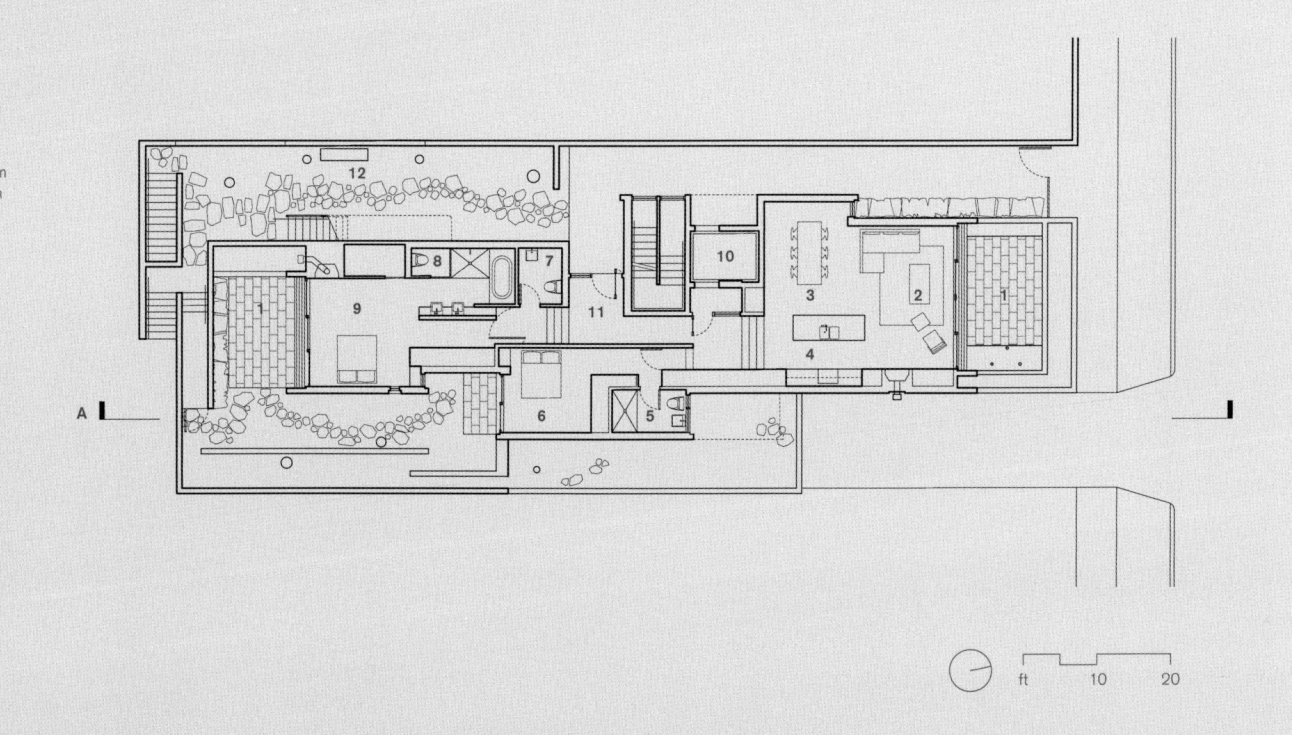

Section A

1. Guest Bedroom
2. Guest Bathroom
3. Powder Room
4. Parking Garage

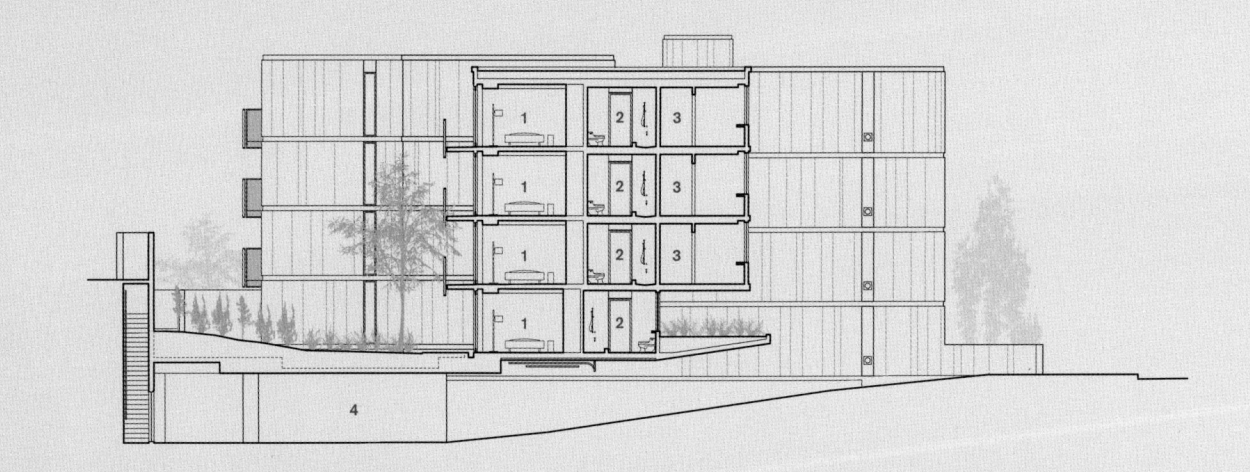

39

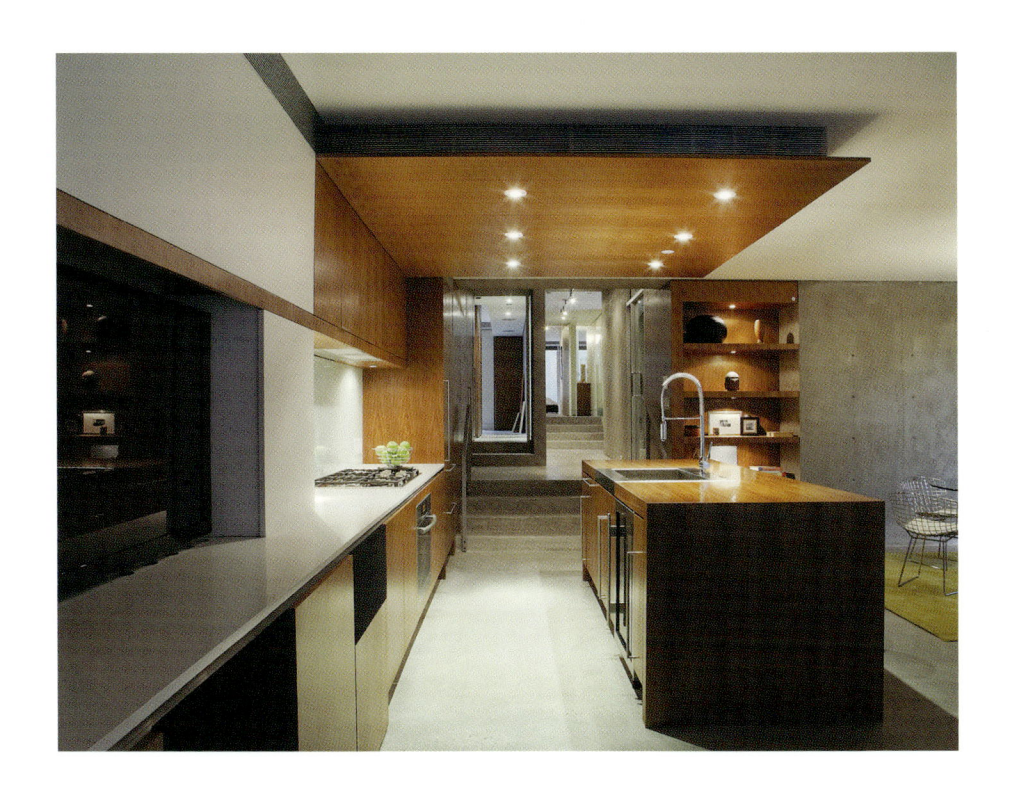

Gambier 1

Building Area
2000 ft² (185 m²)

Location
Gambier Island, British Columbia

Building Type
Vacation home

Year
2007

The cabin is located on a site defined by a dramatic four-storey rock face that rises directly out of the ocean. Focused around a moss covered rock outcropping, the site has a thick ground cover of ferns and salal. Dense stands of existing trees — arbutus, fir, and cedar — frame views to the east over Howe Sound and to the North Shore Mountains. Access to the site is by boat.

This remote site, characterized by its spectacular setting, is not serviced and consequently the design was developed to incorporate sustainable strategies. The plan organizes the cabin's living spaces along a meandering path that links the saltwater dock to the island forest. Dwelling spaces in the cabin acquaint inhabitants with the extent, landform, and vegetation of the site. The path also defines a courtyard at the centre of the house which surrounds a moss-covered granite outcrop. Expansive views towards the south also allow natural daylight into the heart of the cabin.

To minimize the disturbance to natural landscapes, the building is detailed to reduce the impact of construction. The floor slab was cantilevered from the foundations to minimize the footings, while walls and other building assemblies were prefabricated off site.

The cabin is clad in beveled cedar siding stained black and installed vertically in a random pattern, lending the cladding a bark-like quality that recalls the conifers on the site. This envelope also creates overhangs to define a series of hooded outdoor spaces. These intermediate zones, offering protection from the rain and an expanded threshold between inside and out, are lined with locally milled red cedar siding and hemlock soffits which contrast with the dark block of the house, and add a warm glow that echoes the red bark of the surrounding arbutus trees.

Main Floor

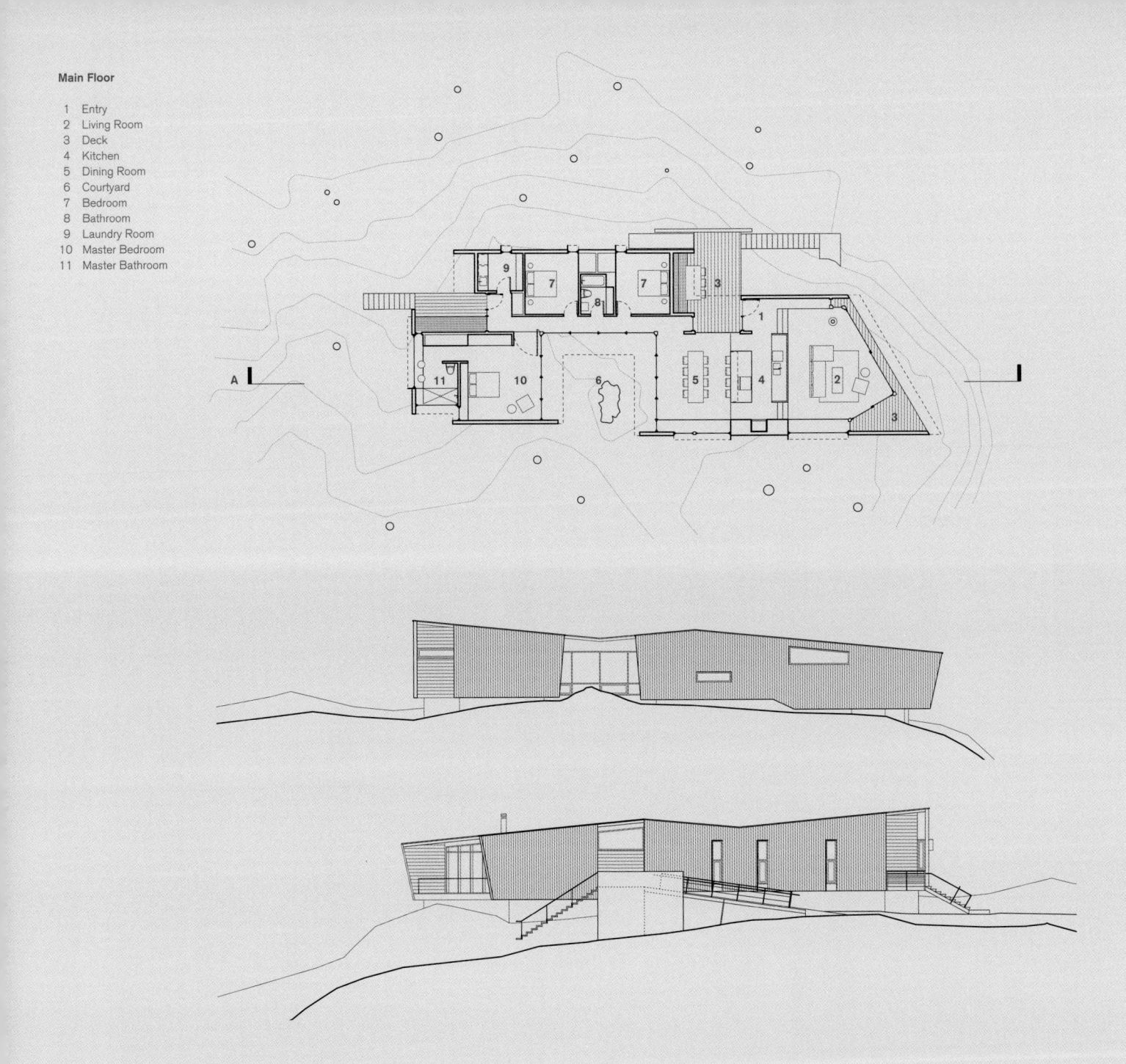

1. Entry
2. Living Room
3. Deck
4. Kitchen
5. Dining Room
6. Courtyard
7. Bedroom
8. Bathroom
9. Laundry Room
10. Master Bedroom
11. Master Bathroom

ft 20 50

43

ft 20 50

44

Section A

   1   Living Room
   2   Kitchen
   3   Dining Room
   4   Courtyard
   5   Master Bedroom
   6   Master Bathroom

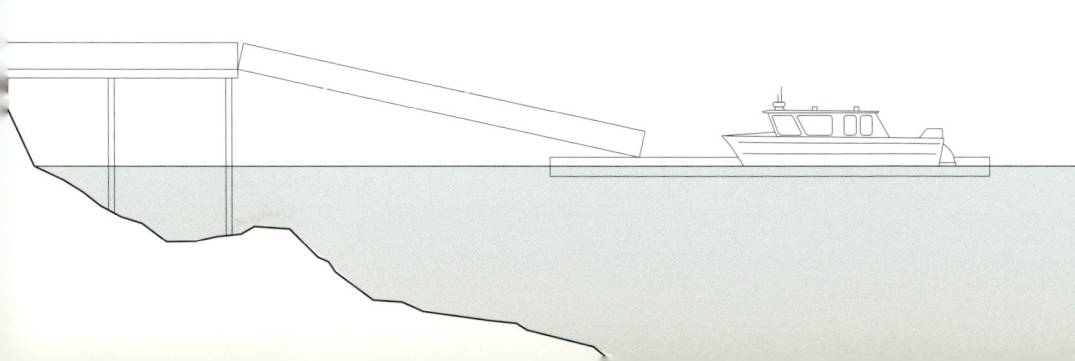

46

47

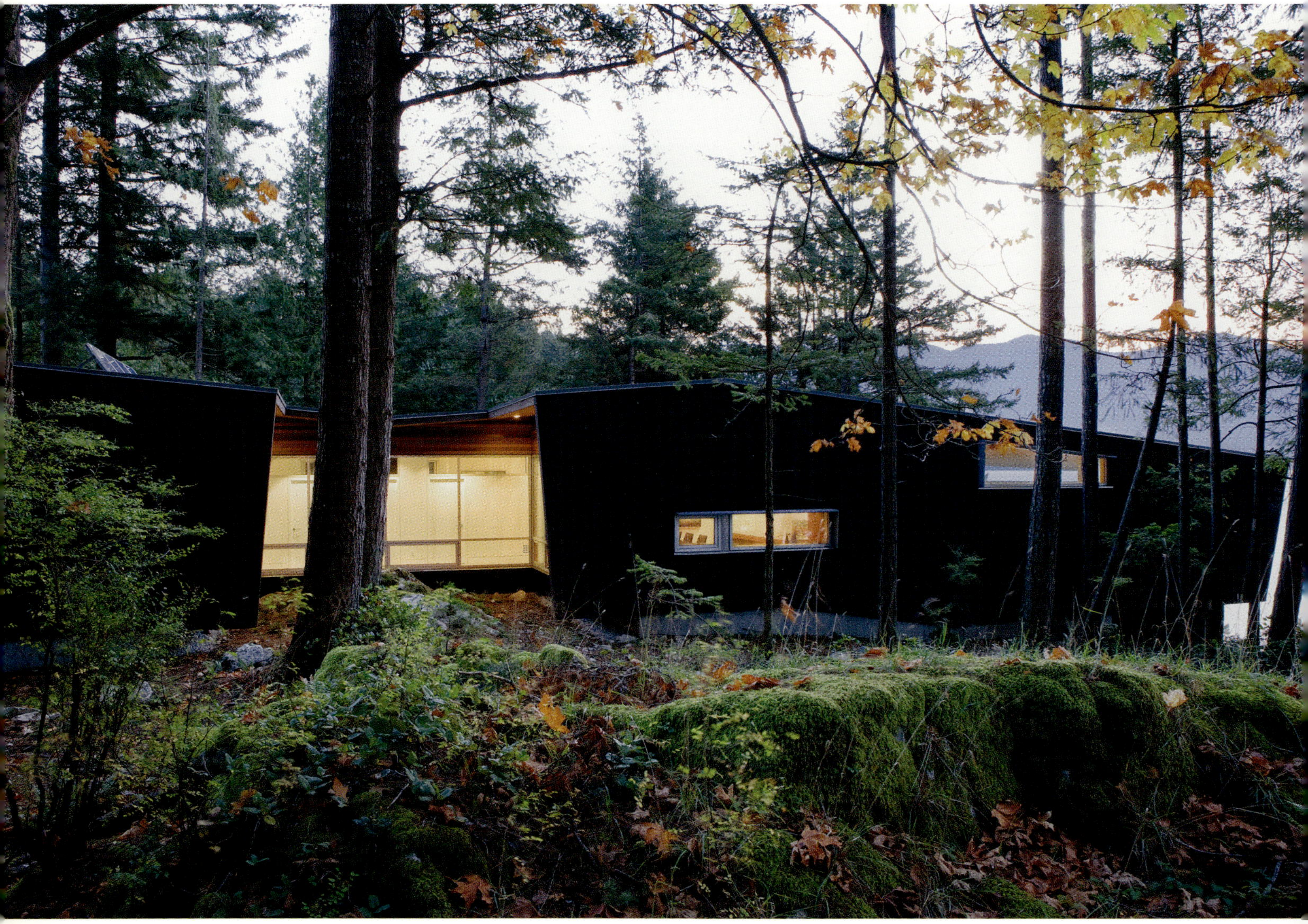

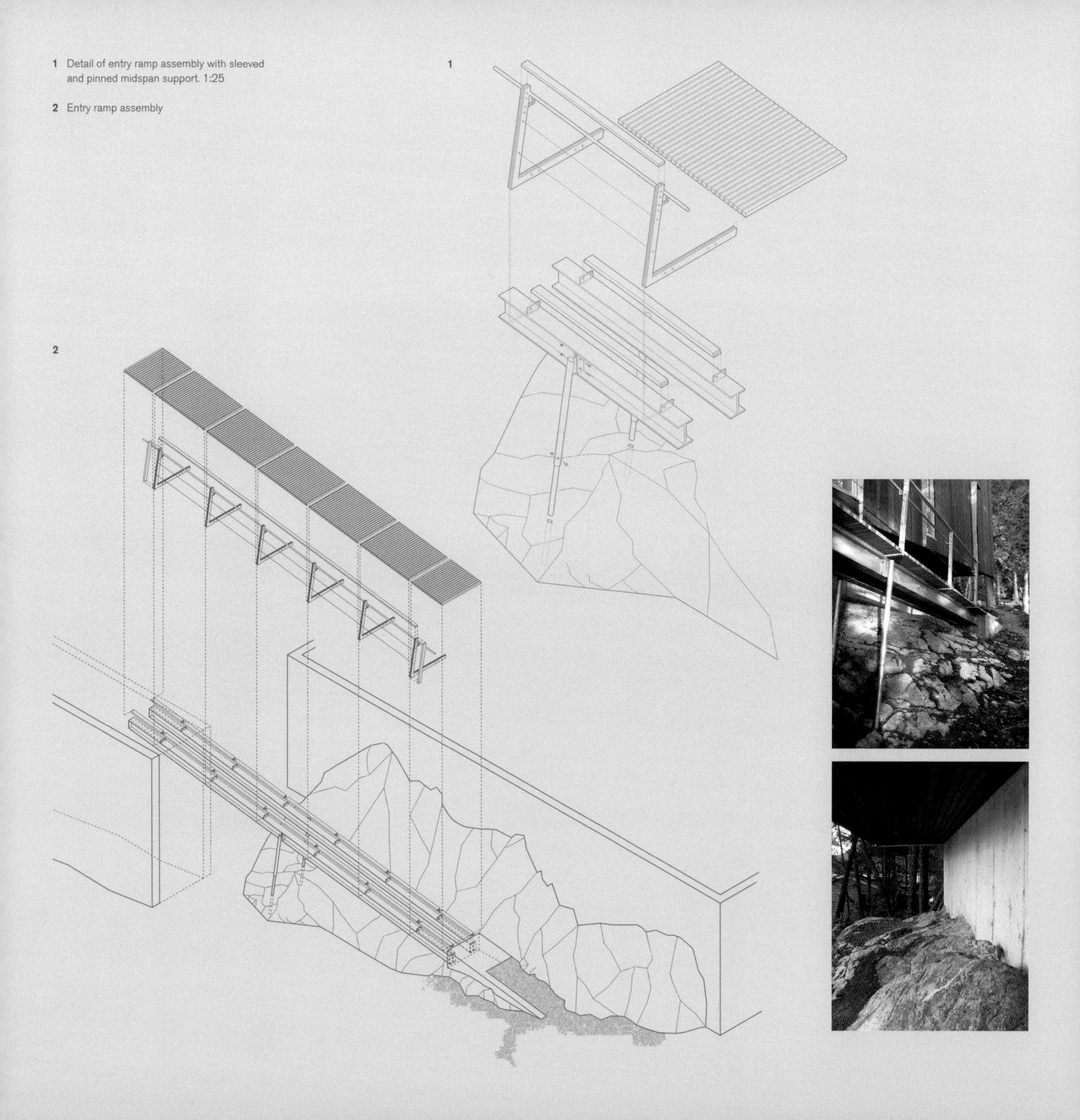

1 Detail of entry ramp assembly with sleeved and pinned midspan support. 1:25

2 Entry ramp assembly

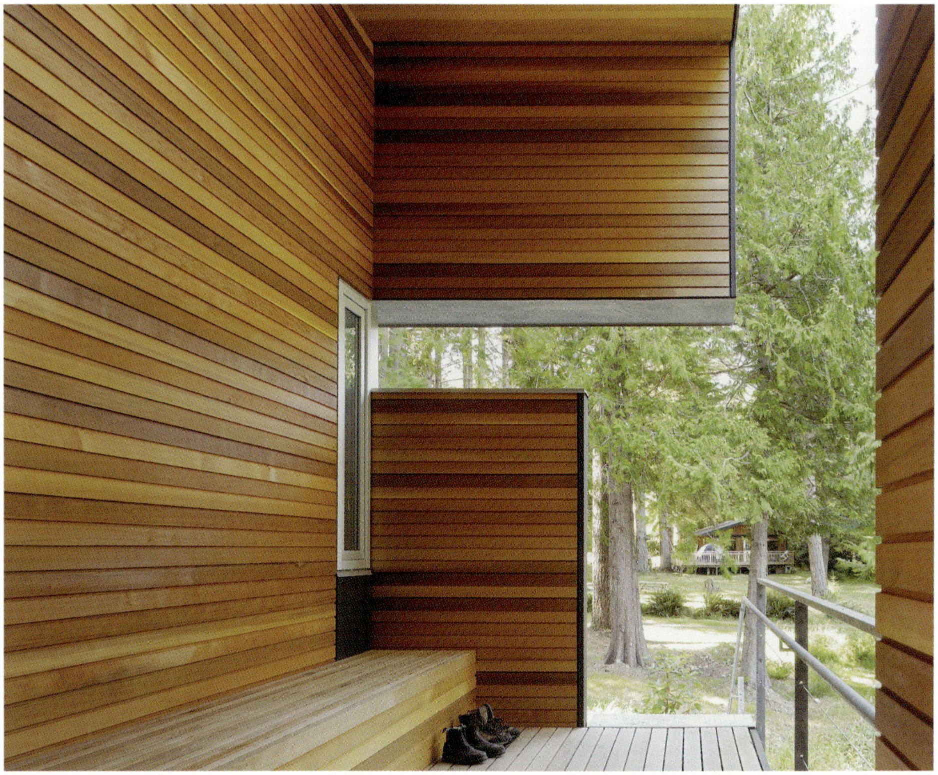

51

Tolmie

Building Area
3200 ft² (300 m²)

Location
Vancouver, British Columbia

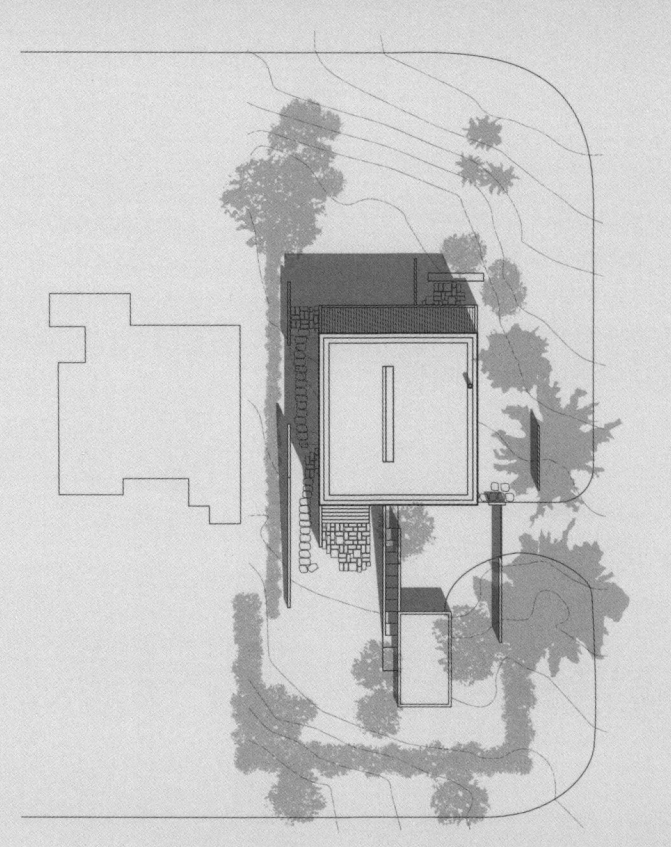

Building Type
Single-family residence

Year
2008

The house was planned to provide privacy for a single family within a busy urban waterfront setting in Vancouver. Landscaping and grading are used to frame views of the water and North Shore Mountains beyond while at the same time defining access and maintaining informal connections to the surroundings on the site. By contrast, spaces on the lower level are organized to engage with the immediate landscape and planting.

The design seeks to merge landscape and building. A field of concrete walls at grade frame the landscape, forming outdoor courtyards and providing a foundation for the woodclad upper storey. The roof of the carport is an elevated garden linked by an outdoor path to the house. Inside the dwelling, a central concrete wall brings light down the stair hall and into the living spaces.

The corners of the building are eroded to blur the boundaries between indoor and outdoor spaces, while windows are strategically placed to offer specific views of the site. For example, a desk in the office appears contiguous with a dense mat of groundcover while a high window in the bathroom captures light filtered by an adjacent bamboo hedge.

Lower Floor

1. Storage
2. Carport
3. Entry
4. Mechanical Room
5. Sitting Room
6. Family Room
7. Office / Bedroom
8. Bathroom
9. Bedroom

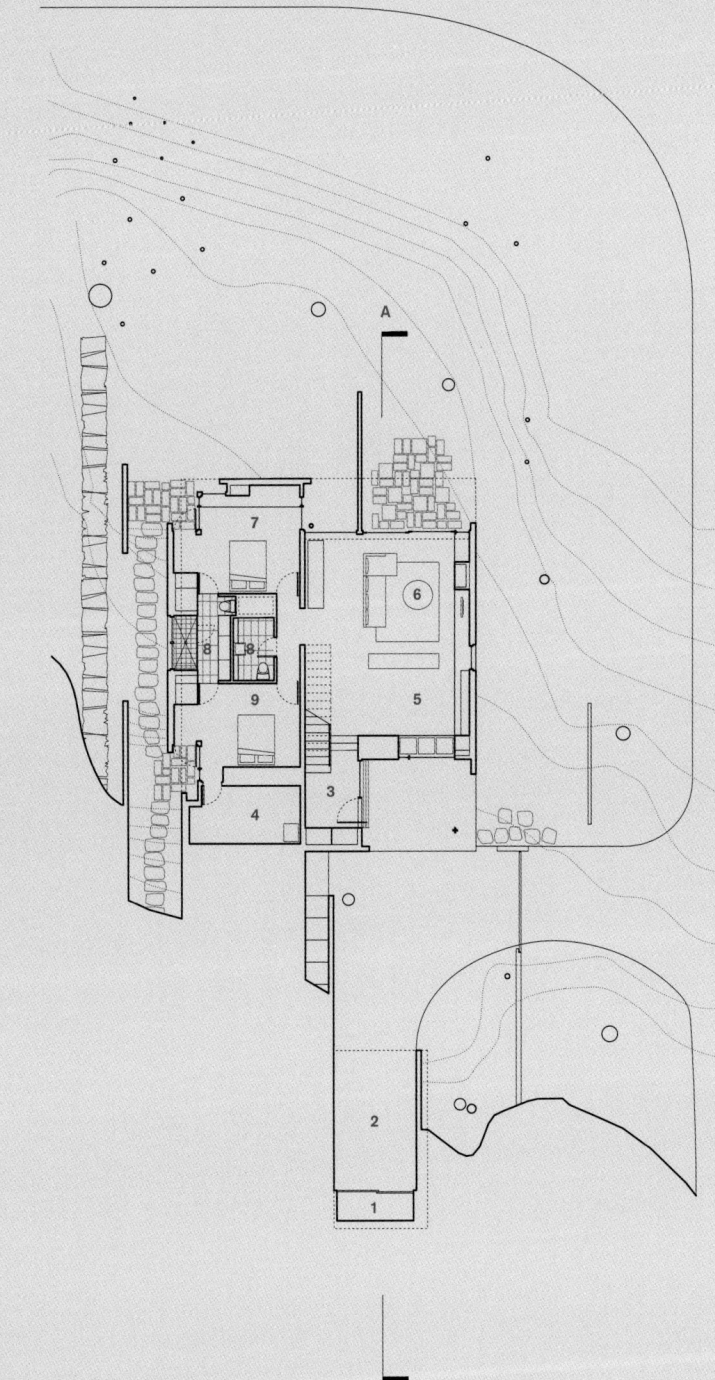

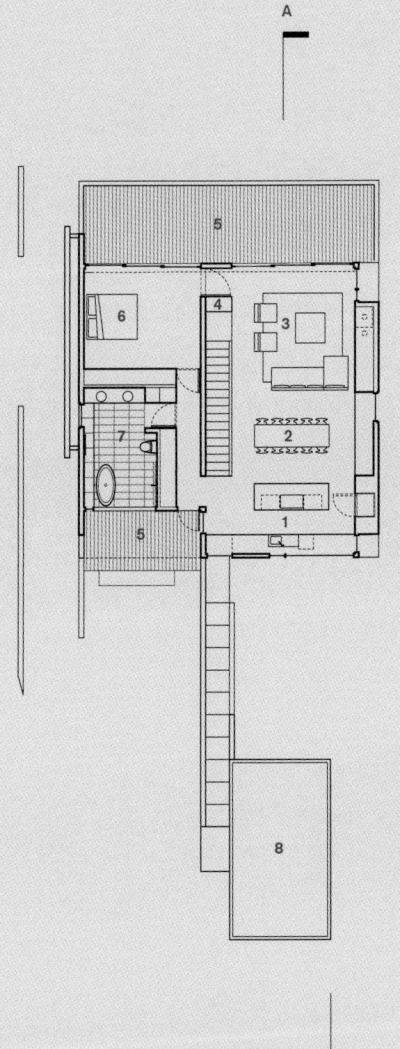

Upper Floor

1. Kitchen
2. Dining Room
3. Living Room
4. Display Ledge
5. Deck
6. Master Bedroom
7. Master Bathroom
8. Planted Roof

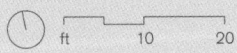

ft 10 20

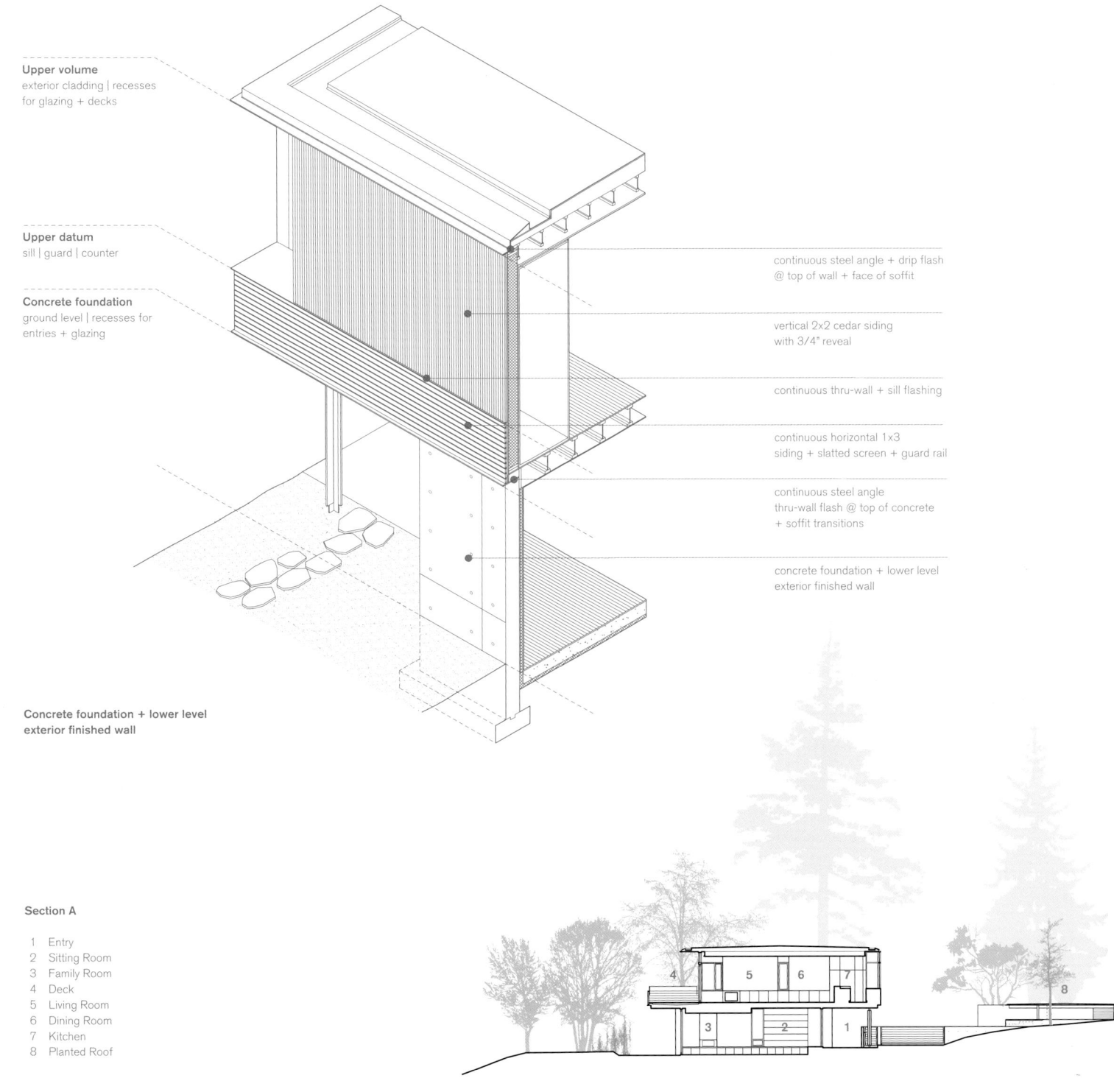

Upper volume
exterior cladding | recesses
for glazing + decks

Upper datum
sill | guard | counter

Concrete foundation
ground level | recesses for
entries + glazing

continuous steel angle + drip flash
@ top of wall + face of soffit

vertical 2x2 cedar siding
with 3/4" reveal

continuous thru-wall + sill flashing

continuous horizontal 1x3
siding + slatted screen + guard rail

continuous steel angle
thru-wall flash @ top of concrete
+ soffit transitions

concrete foundation + lower level
exterior finished wall

Concrete foundation + lower level
exterior finished wall

Section A

1 Entry
2 Sitting Room
3 Family Room
4 Deck
5 Living Room
6 Dining Room
7 Kitchen
8 Planted Roof

56

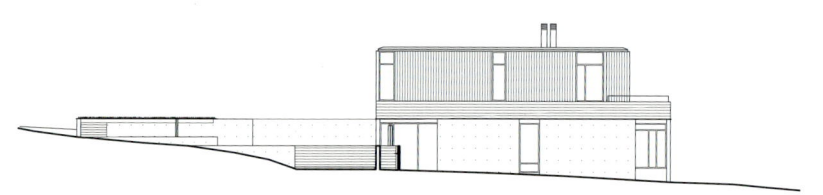

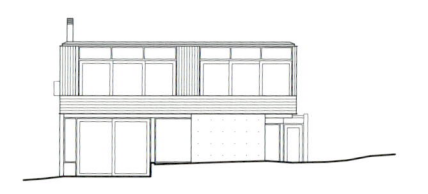

57

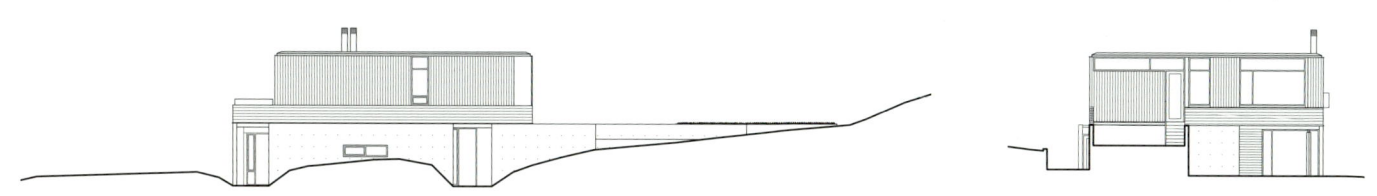

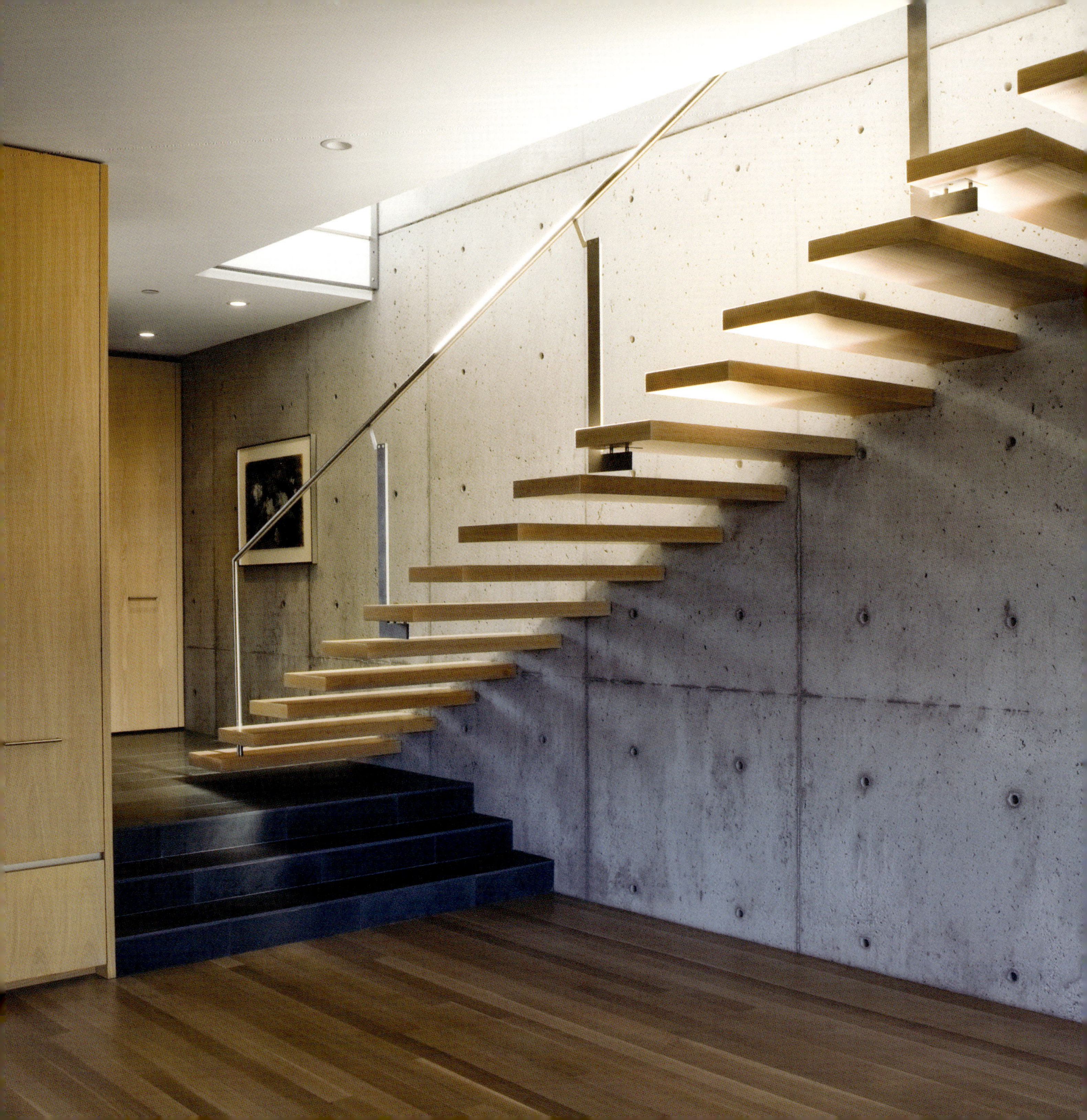

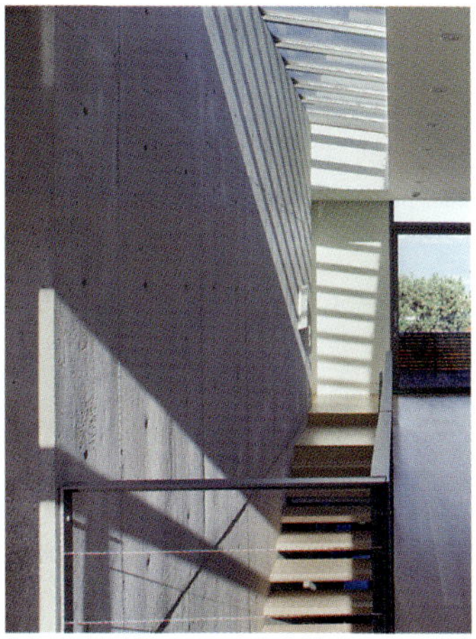

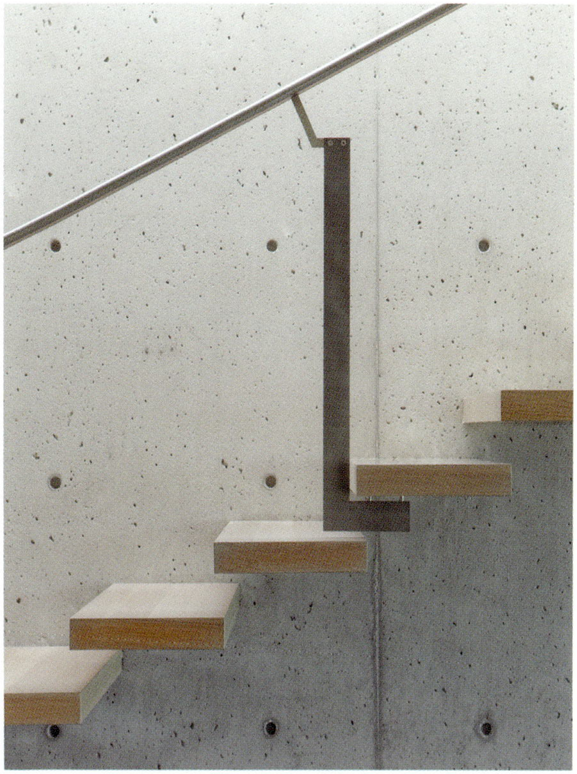

Whistler

Building Area
5800 ft² (540 m²)

Location
Whistler, British Columbia

Building Type
Single-family residence

Year
2010

Located in an expanding neighborhood of large-scale homes on a slope above the resort community of Whistler, British Columbia, this house occupies a restrictive, yet prominent, site in the development. The visual mass of this large volume is minimized by strategic use of the terrain and careful blasting of the bedrock. As such, a substantial portion of the house appears below grade. The thoughtful allocation of program results in a home that is extremely private without compromising access to daylight and panoramic views.

In the often garish context of Whistler vacation homes, the design consisted of a structure that captures the essential qualities of the 'ski lodge' but without the typical formal and stylistic constraints. The lowest level, which connects directly to grade, has a maze-like disposition of private and communal spaces. Exposed concrete walls bracket seamless wood lined alcoves that provide access to the sleeping quarters and service spaces located on this level. The main floor is a large open room with multiple natural light sources and varied views to the forest and mountains beyond. Walls extend past corners expanding the dwelling space into a larger field. Outside walls further increase the perceptual limits of the interior, while cropping views to control exposure and provide privacy.

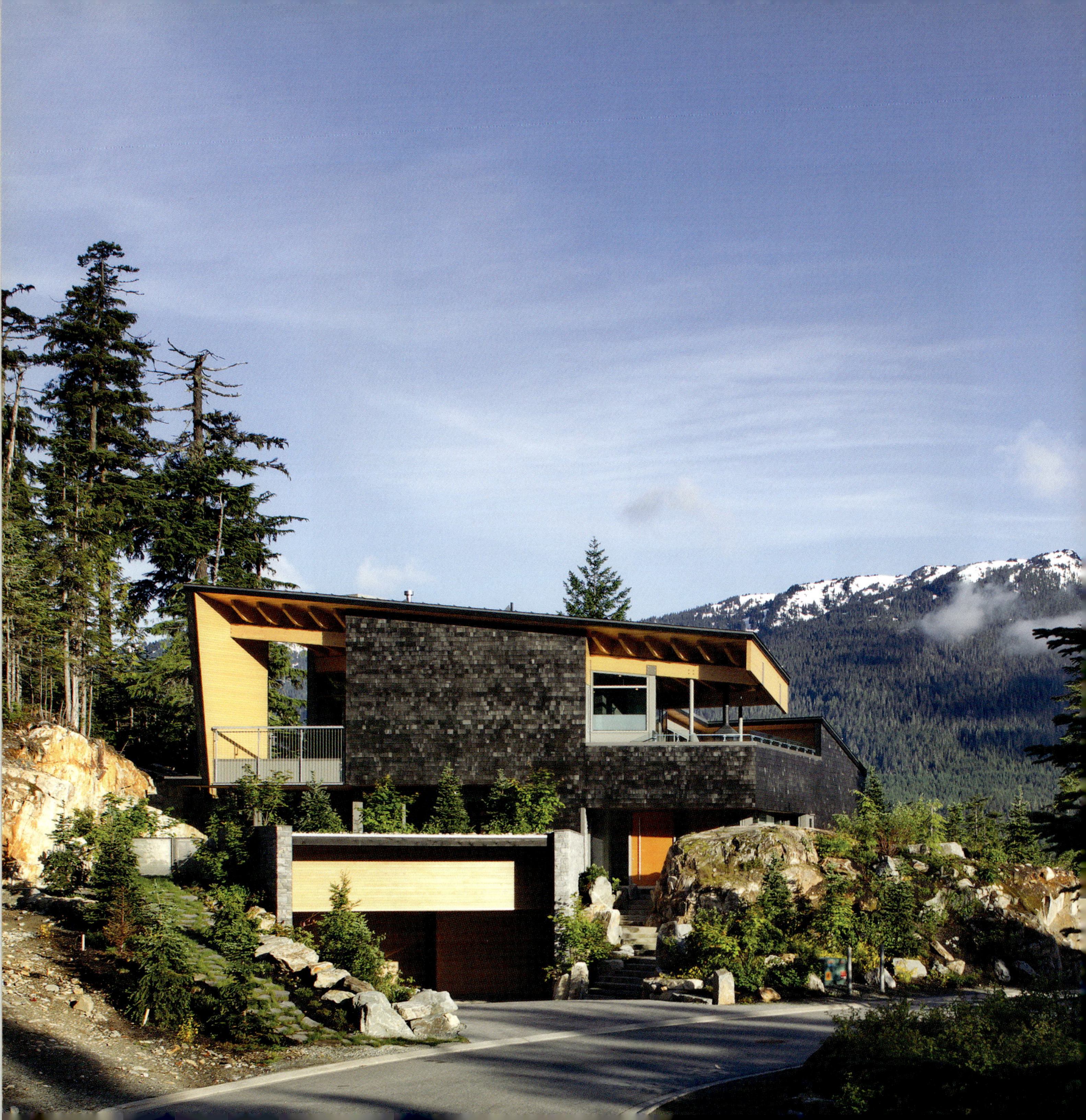

Section

1 Deck
2 Master Bedroom
3 Barbeque Area
4 Living Room
5 Dining Room
6 Kitchen
7 Garage
8 Crawl Space
9 Bedroom 1
10 Bedroom 2
11 Terrace

65

Salt Spring Island

The house is situated at the base of a rock outcropping with an entrance from a wide stair that leads between the outcropping and an angled concrete wall to an entry courtyard framed by the building and a grove of arbutus trees. A shed roof, aligned with the slope of the land, slices through a series of walls. A courtyard plan separates guest rooms from private living areas and the master bedroom suite. Connections to the landscape — both near and far — are realized through a series of cuts and folds which integrate the building with its surroundings. The buildings are clad in grey-stained cedar while red-stained plywood cladding highlights the cuts that have been made into the body of the house.

Building Area
3000 ft² (275 m²)

Location
Salt Spring Island, British Columbia

Building Type
Vacation home

Year
2011

Main Floor

1. Entry
2. Living Room
3. Dining Room
4. Kitchen
5. Master Bedroom
6. Master Bathroom
7. Bathroom
8. Office
9. Bedroom
10. Garage
11. Deck
12. Arbutus Grove

Section A

1. Living / Dining
2. Kitchen
3. Crawl Space
4. Garage
5. Guest House Bedroom
6. Deck

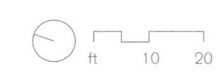

Overlap   Overlap

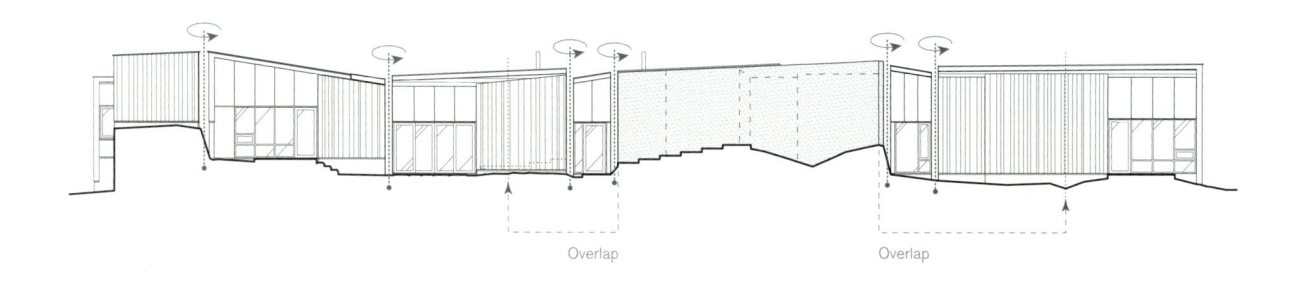

69

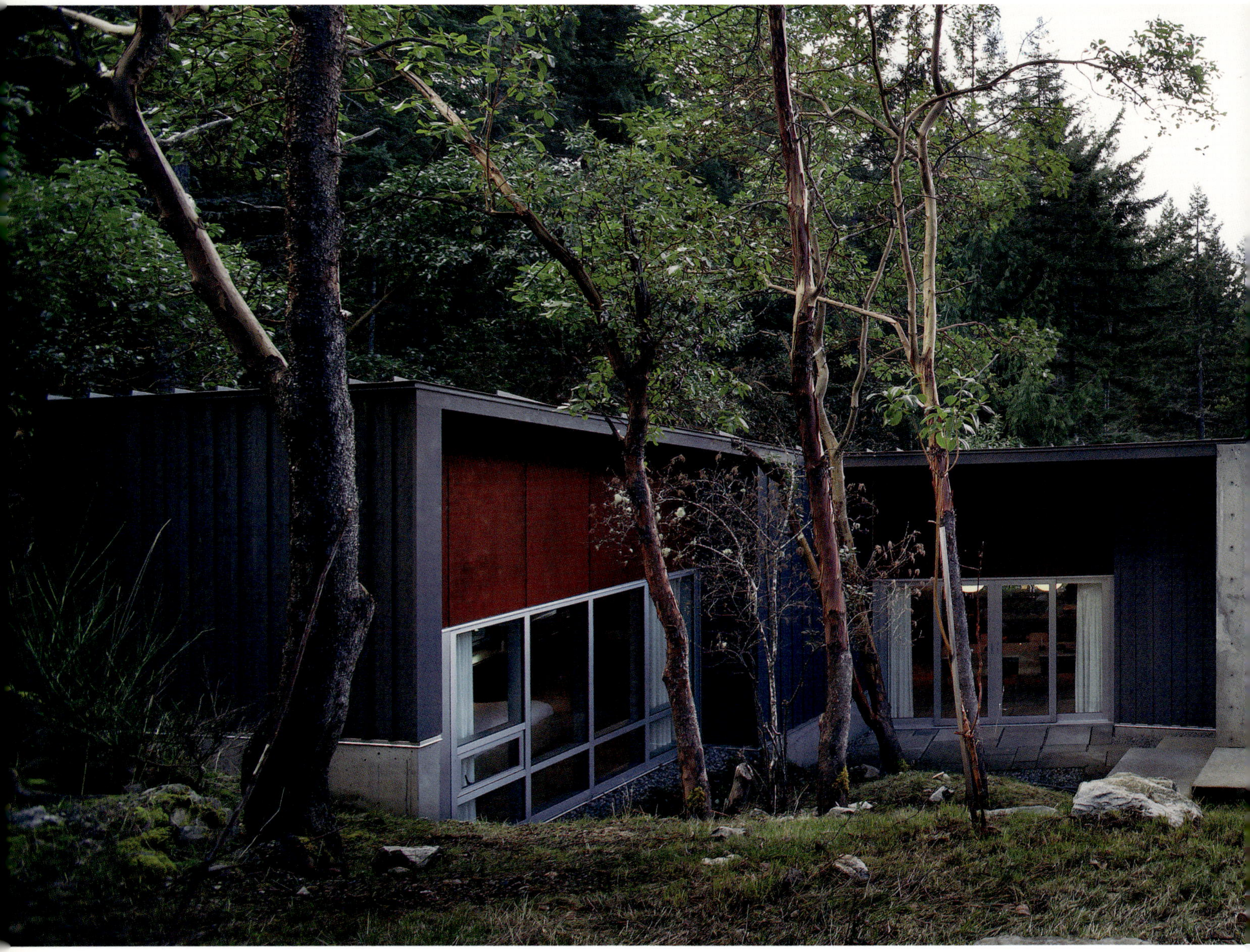

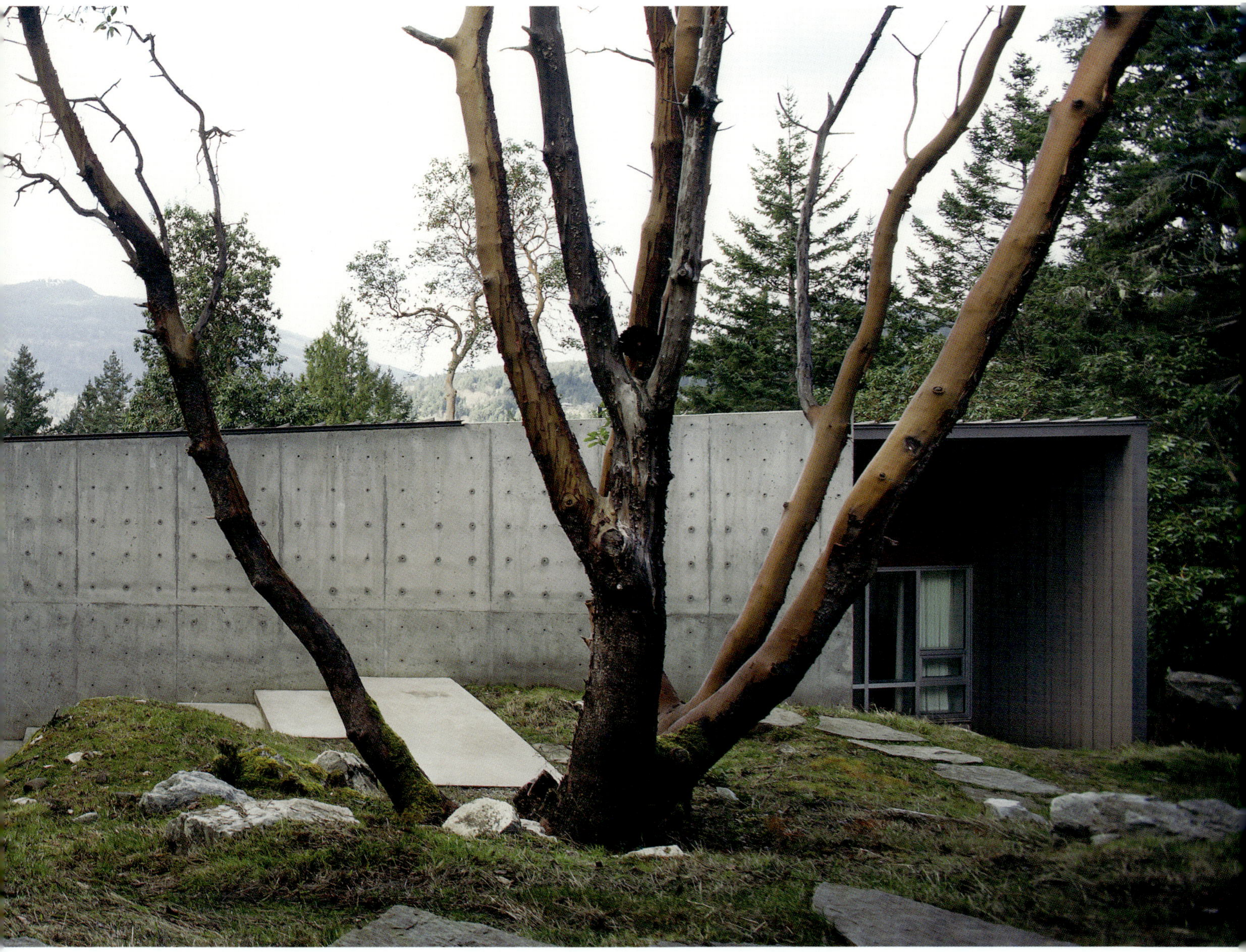

Gambier 2

Building Area
3500 ft² (325 m²)

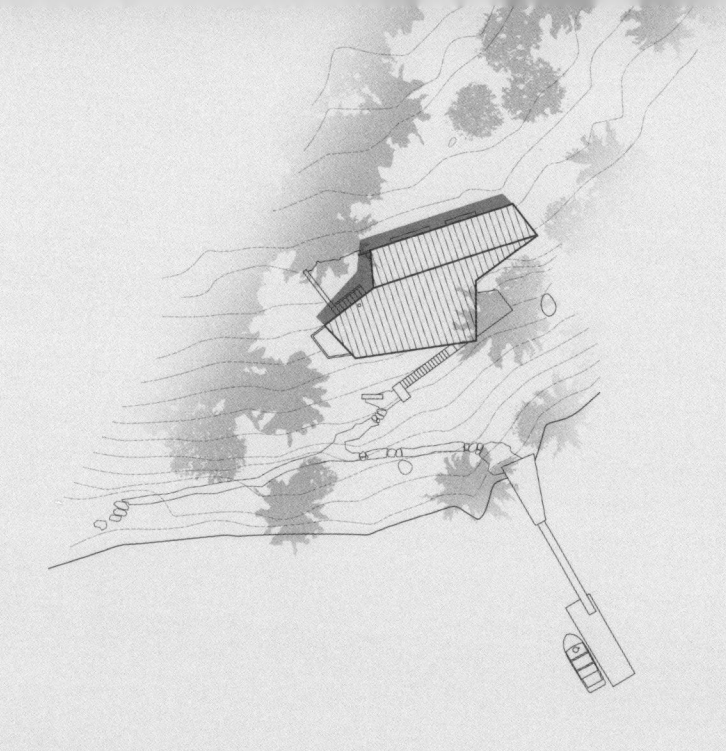

Location
Gambier Island, British Columbia

Building Type
Vacation residence

Year
2011

Explorations of this steeply sloped, wooded site overlooking a small private stone beach in Center Bay suggested a switchback organization of spaces where the slope has been extended and combined with the introduction of a meandering path that traverses the site. This pathway purposefully links together the architecture of internal rooms and outdoor spaces with discoveries of the site's varied landscape.

One third of the space within the house, made up of guest rooms, an office and the main entrance, is located at the lower level adjacent to the base of a large rock embankment. The overhanging mass of the building and its canted wall define the main entrance and create a covered space for unpacking and packing—a familiar cabin ritual associated with those important moments of arrival and departure. A vertical strip of glazing at the entry and lower stair landing captures the full height of a lone arbutus tree. Family spaces are on the upper level. An internal stair rises up alongside a central concrete wall that extends the rock embankment into the house's internal landscape. This wall supports cantilevered roof rafters which form a ridge centered over the stair hall. Windows and sliding doors in the family areas upstairs open for ventilation and frame elements of the natural surrounds: the expansive southwest water views, the foliage of an arbutus tree, the steep rock bluff adjacent to a terrace. The switchback path continues to the children's bedrooms with intimate views of the rocky hillside, and arrives finally at the master bedroom, where a cantilevered glazed end wall frames the fragile landscape of a moss-and wildflower-covered clearing.

Lower Floor

1. Entry
2. Hallway
3. Study
4. Guest Bedroom
5. Guest Bathroom
6. Terrace
7. Mechanical Room

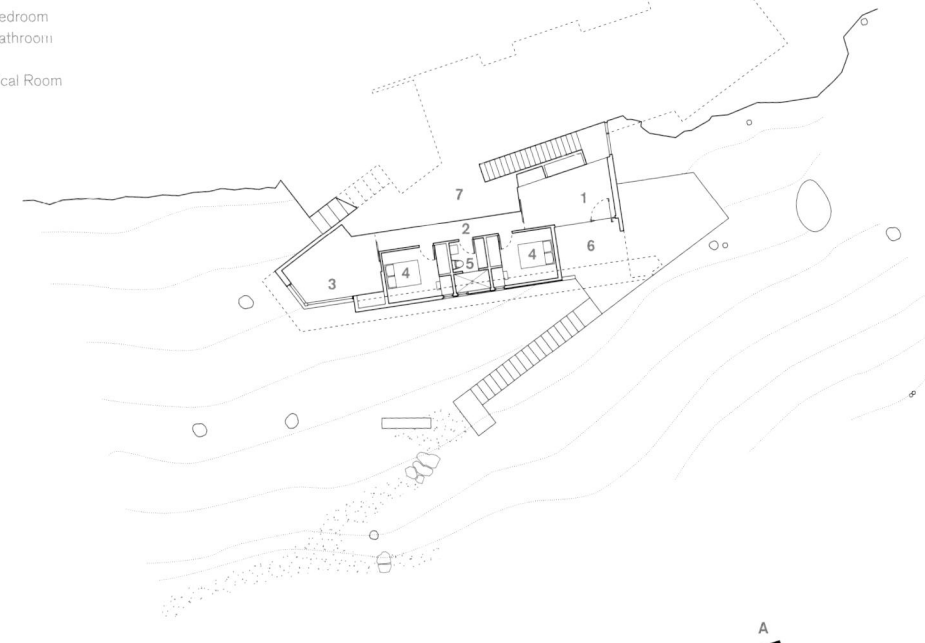

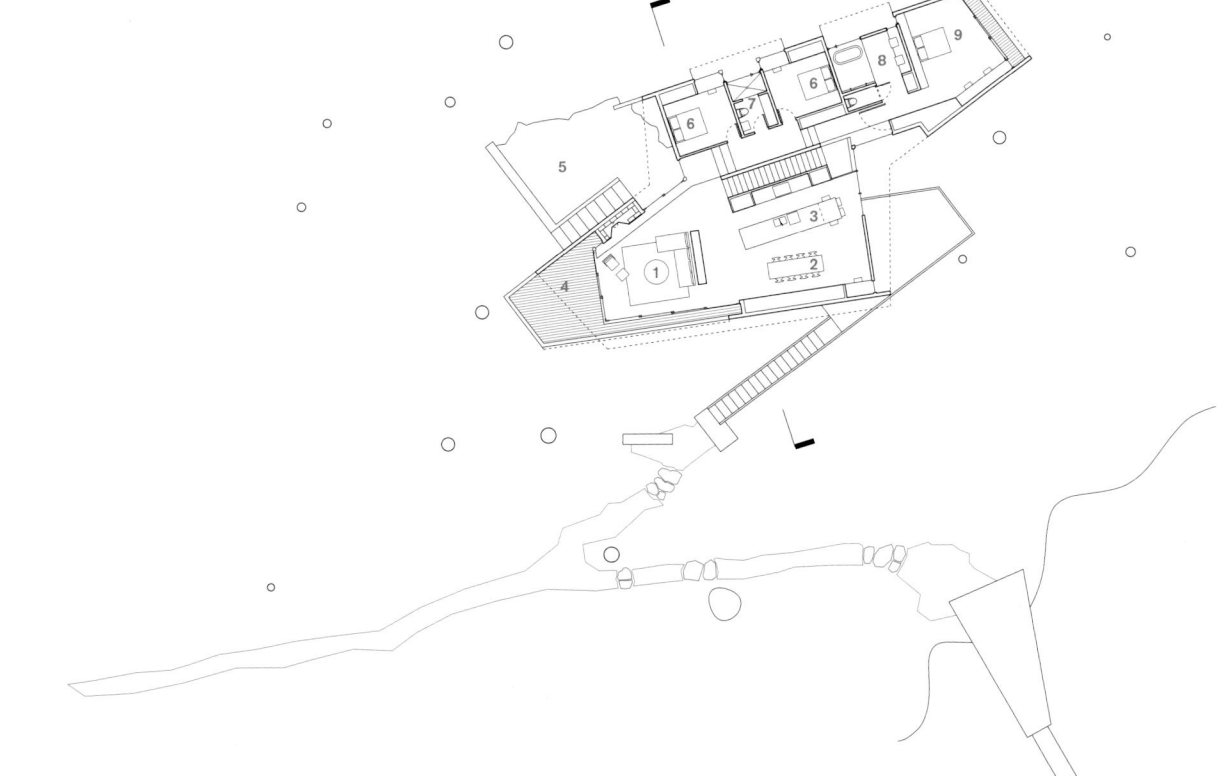

Main Floor

1. Living Room
2. Dining Room
3. Kitchen
4. Deck
5. Terrace
6. Bedroom
7. Bathroom
8. Master Bathroom
9. Master Bedroom

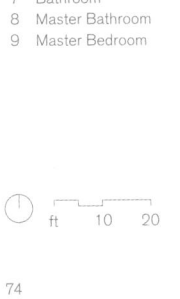

ft 10 20

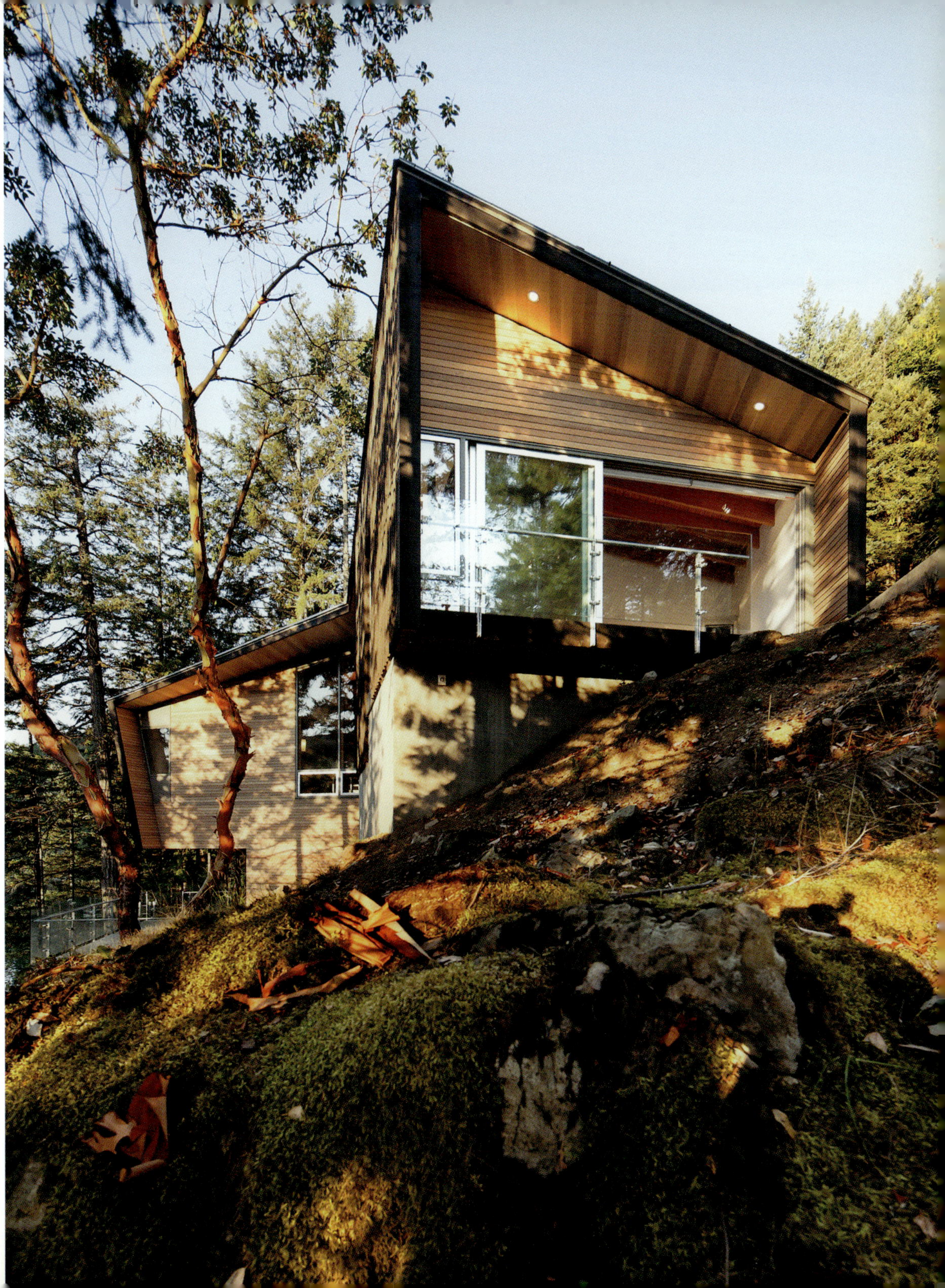

Section A

1 Guest Shower
2 Deck
3 Dining Room
4 Kitchen
5 Hall
6 Bedroom

77

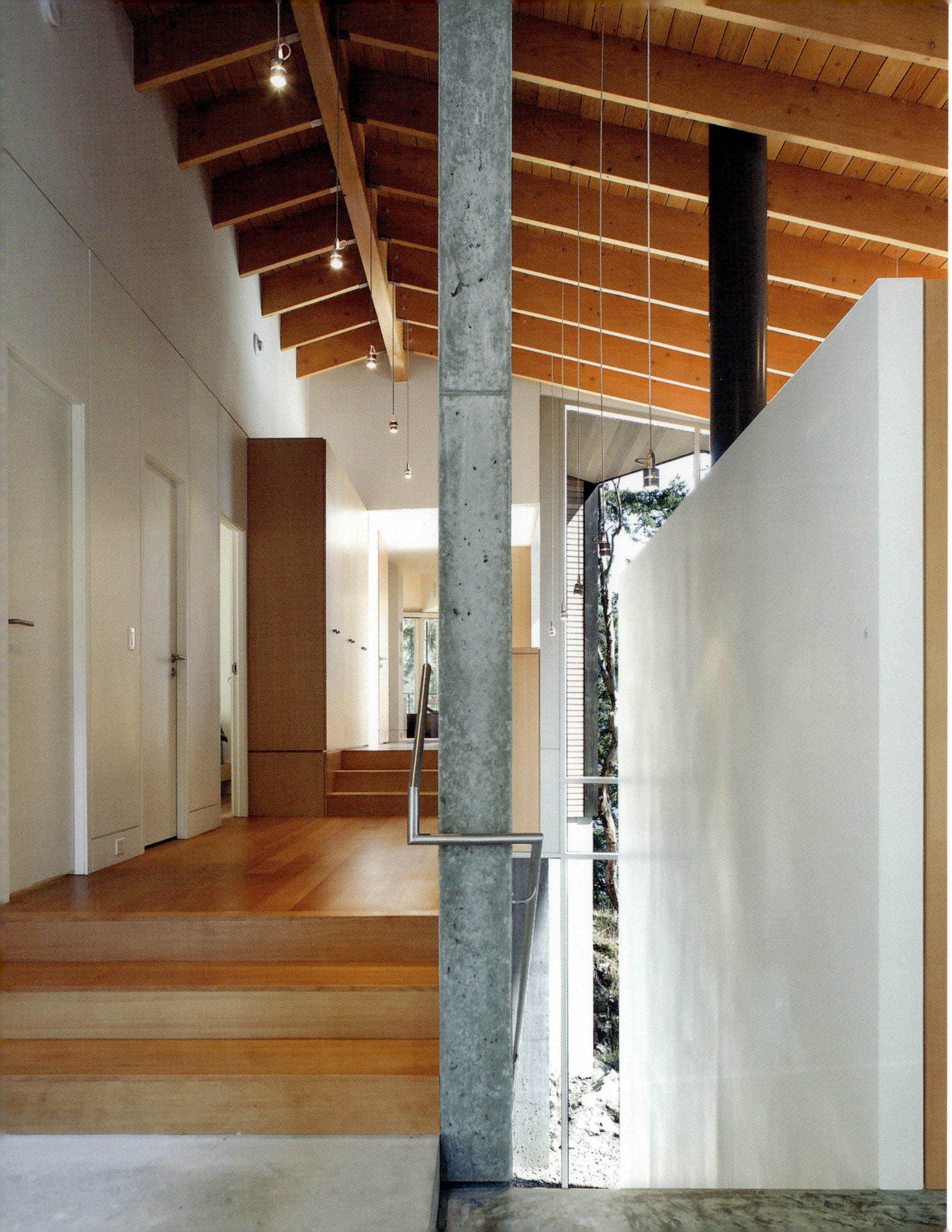

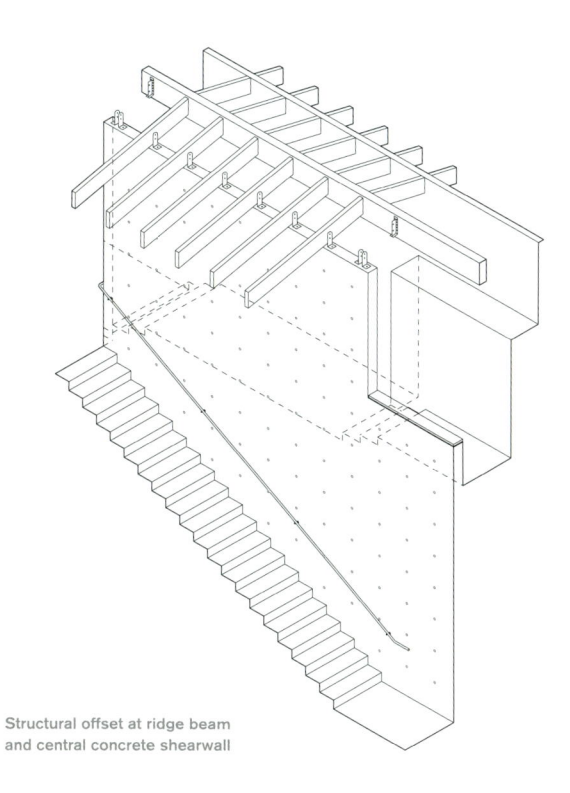

Structural offset at ridge beam
and central concrete shearwall

79

Fairmile

Building Area
4600 ft² (425 m²)

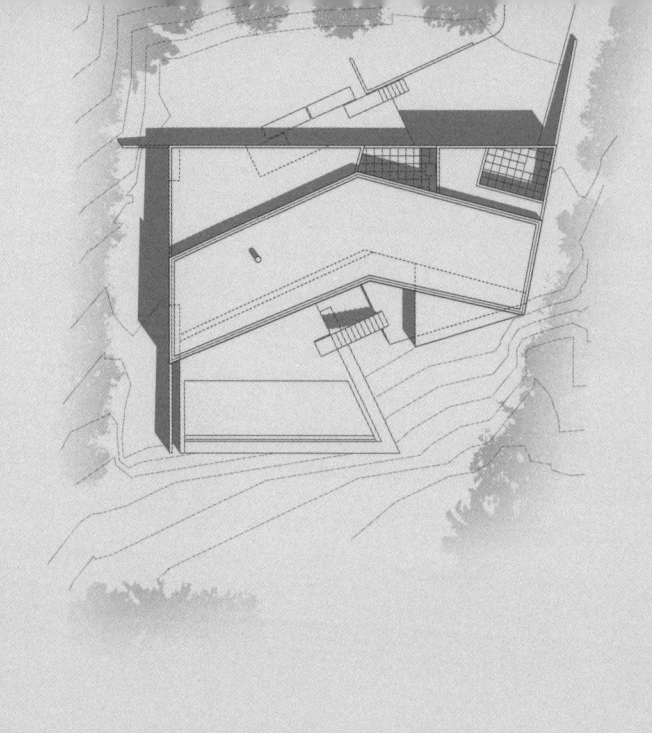

Location
West Vancouver, British Columbia

Building Type
Single-family residence

Year
2011

A series of basic transformations to a simple form exploit the wide frontage and southern exposure of this steep site. Within the home, a diverse experiential sequence focuses on privacy, light, and liveability. The box was initially formed in response to municipal setback requirements. A raised portion of the main roof over the living spaces expands exposure to sunlight and southern views while incorporating north-facing automated clerestory windows for ventilation. This 'lifted' roof is manipulated internally to drop into the box form, respond to structural spanning, and create angled planes that bounce light into the core of the house. A bend in the south-facing volume provides privacy from neighboring properties and differentiates the south-easterly view to the City of Vancouver and Lion's Gate Bridge from west-facing views towards the Georgia Strait and Gulf Islands. Floors extending south create outdoor terraces that screen further development down the slope. The extension of the east and west side walls and substantial roof overhangs offer additional privacy, while mitigating solar gains. Two north-facing courtyards offer respite from the sunny south terraces while improving ventilation and natural light. These private outdoor rooms also serve as sculpture gardens. The lower roof will be planted with a tall indigenous grass mix visible from the road and living spaces, while an upper roof will be covered with a low lying succulent layer to protect the roof membrane, reduce heat reflectivity, and minimize rain overflow into municipal systems. Board-formed concrete contrasts with the smooth anodized aluminum and back-painted glass. These surfaces on external soffits, infill panels, and frameless windows reflect the lush vegetation on the site and sunlight from the pool, while tracing ever changing seasonal shifts.

82

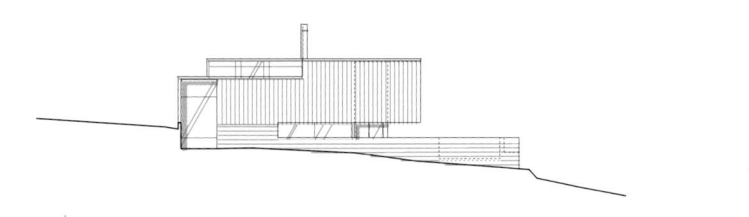

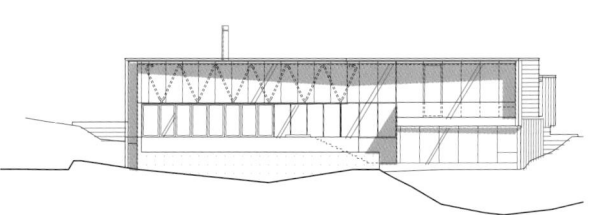

Main Floor

1. Entry
2. Living Room
3. Dining
4. Kitchen
5. Master Bedroom
6. Master Ensuite
7. Master Dressing Room
8. Bedroom
9. Bathroom
10. Powder Room
11. Laundry Room
12. Garden Courtyard
13. Terrace
14. Pool
15. Master deck
16. Water Feature

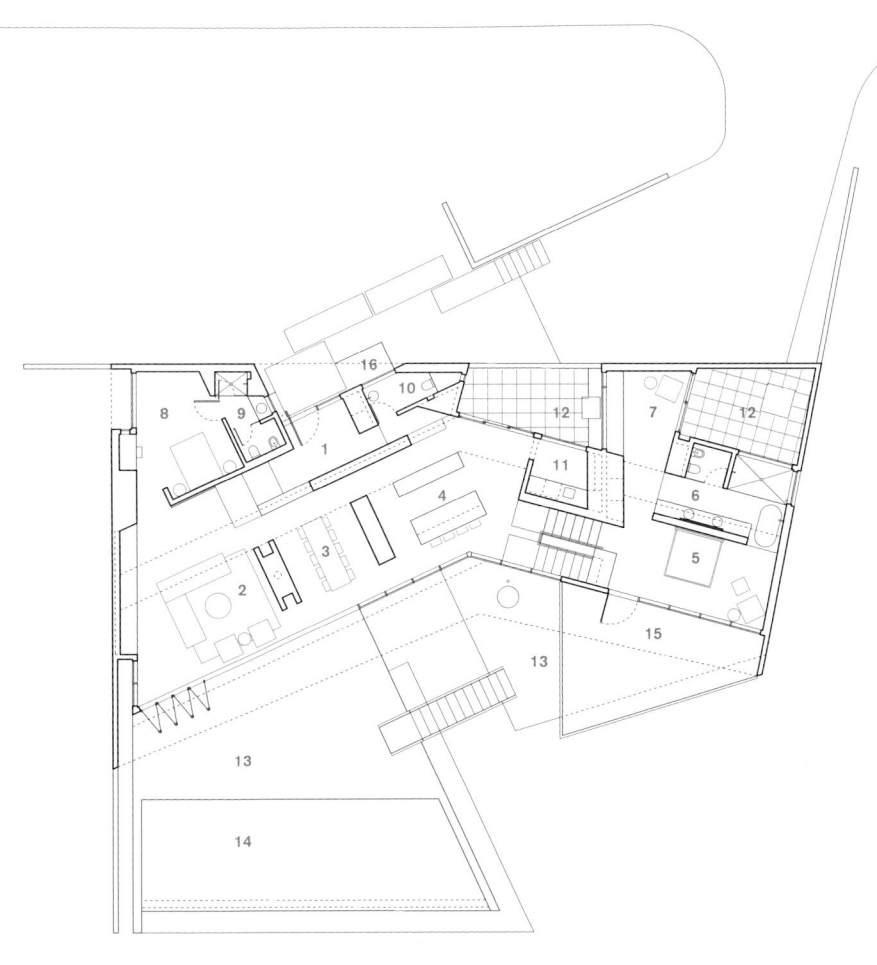

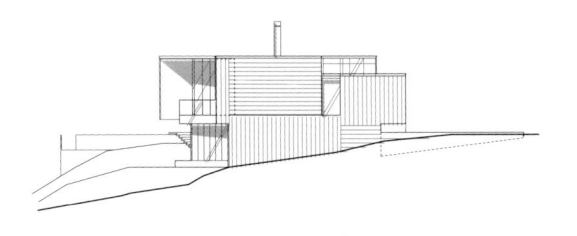

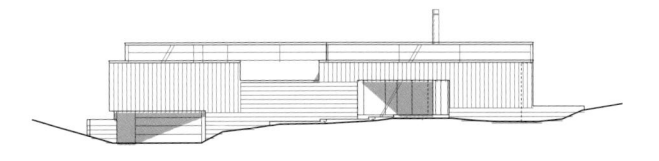

Postscript

Brian Carter

In the course of the preparation of this book, David Battersby and Heather Howat were commissioned to design a new field school for the University of British Columbia's Department of Earth and Ocean Sciences. The site is located near an old gold mine and immediately adjacent to the White Lake Grasslands Protected Area in the interior of southeastern British Columbia. The project is to include residential accommodation for students, faculty, and researchers in addition to workspaces, lecture and dining halls together with storage for equipment. It is a commission that will project their work beyond consideration of the spaces of the house and invite speculation about the nature and form of both field camp and 'academical village' in the twenty-first century. However, unlike the bucolic setting of Jefferson's campus for the University of Virginia, this particular outpost, designed specifically for geological research and the study of the earth, will be constructed in remote natural landscapes of British Columbia. It will require a response to the rigorous demands of necessity as well as promises of new found freedoms. This will be a place created out of the difference between the world we are living in and the world that we want to live in. A place defined by what these two architects have already seen but also by what they are about to see.

In 2013 the field school design was recognized with an Award of Excellence from *Canadian Architect*. Jury member Marie-Chantal Croft noted:

"The relationship between the landscape and buildings is key in this project, and the pavilion approach allows nature to exist between these humanly scaled discrete structures. The form and materiality of the buildings are sensitive to their natural context, and the variations in shape of each pavilion bring a richness to the whole."

Main Floor

1. Map Cabin
2. Covered Porch
3. Entry
4. Accessible Bathroom
5. WC
6. Storage
7. Dining / Lecture Hall
8. Kitchen
9. Dish Washing
10. Storage / Cooler
11. Storage / Cleaning
12. Bathroom
13. Garbage / Recycling
14. Service Entry

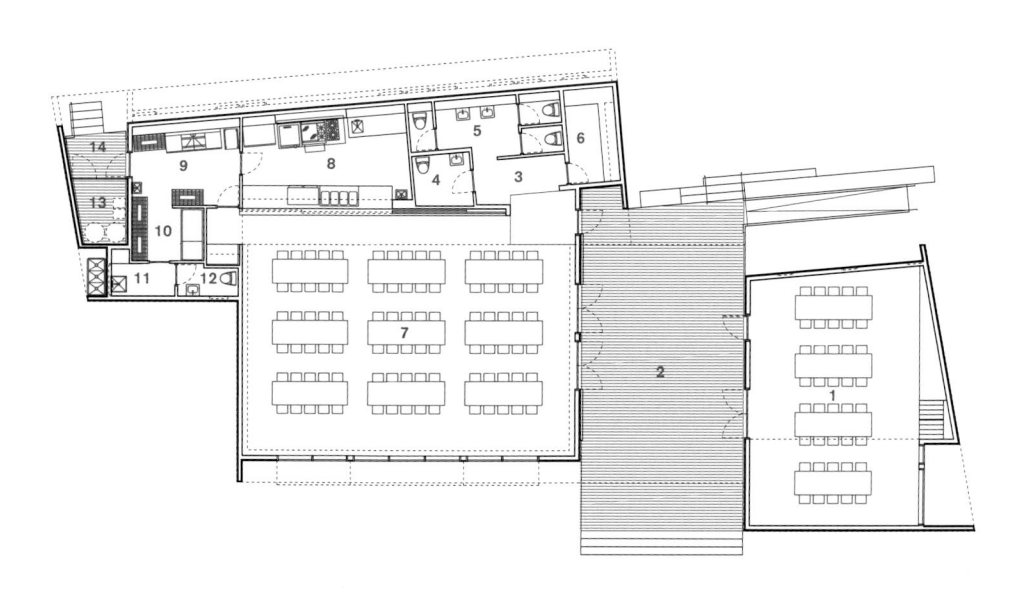

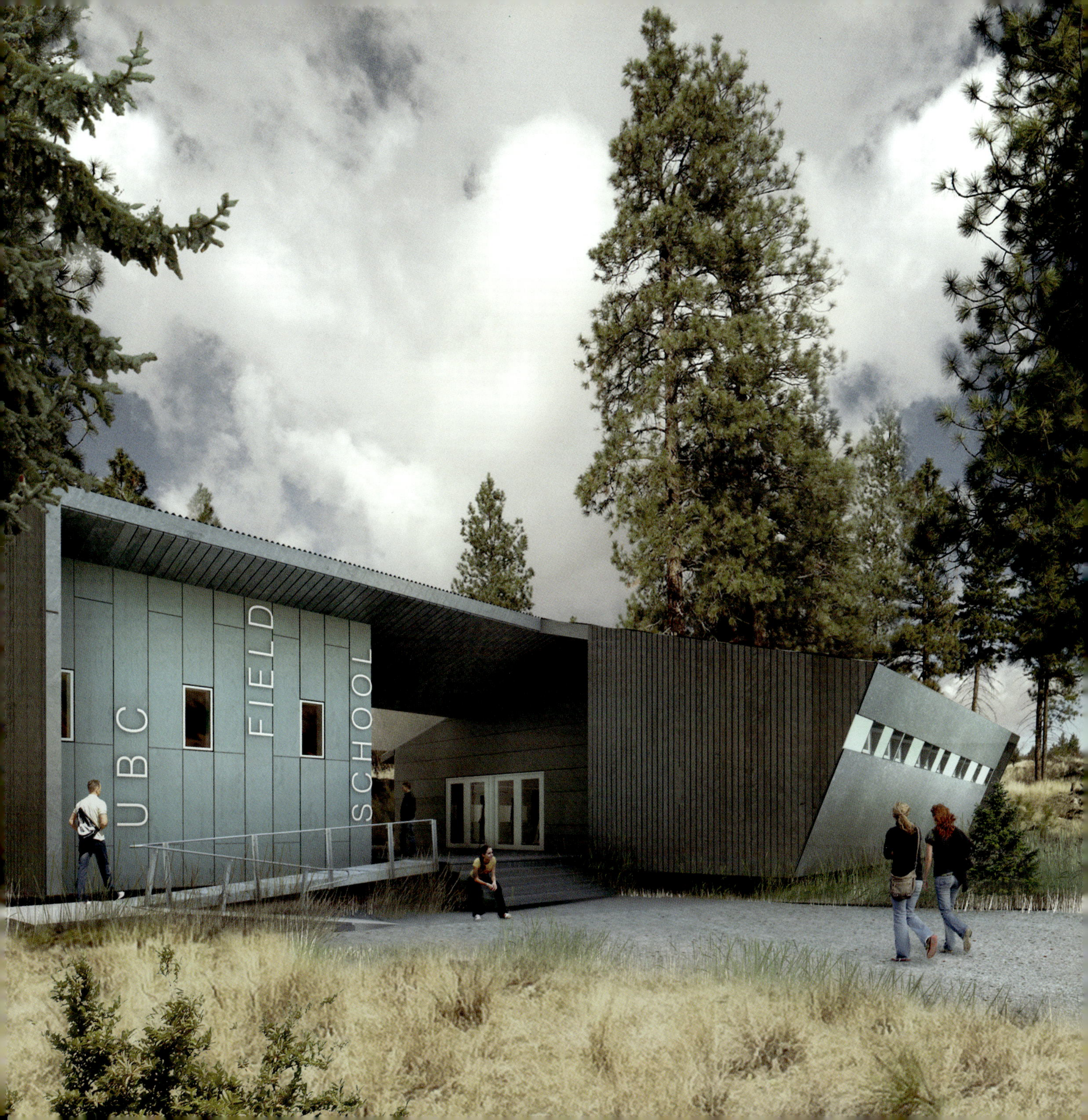
UBC
FIELD
SCHOOL

BattersbyHowat

David Battersby and Heather Howat met at the University of Manitoba where David completed a Bachelor of Environmental Studies (Landscape) degree in 1989 and Heather received her Bachelor of Interior Design degree in 1990. They went on to pursue Master's degrees in Architecture at Dalhousie University and both graduated with honors in 1995. Heather was awarded the Royal Architectural Institute of Canada's Student Gold Medal and David was the recipient of the American Institute of Architects Student Gold Medal.

In 1996, they established the design partnership BattersbyHowat Inc. in Vancouver. They went on to develop that practice and advance a holistic approach to design.

In 2010, BattersbyHowat Architects Inc. was established and the commissioned work has included a series of residences, gardens, art galleries, showrooms and offices as well as furniture and educational facilities.

The work of David Battersby and Heather Howat, which has been published in both national and international professional journals, has also been featured in several books including *Cabin, Cottage and Camp*, *Young Architects Americas*, *A Guidebook to Contemporary Architecture in Vancouver*, *Substance over Spectacle*, *Fundamentals of Sustainable Dwellings*, *West Coast Modern*, and *Houses Now*.

BattersbyHowat was awarded the Ron Thom Award for Early Achievement in Architecture by the Canada Council in 2006 after receiving Canadian Architect Awards of Excellence in 2001 and 2004. In addition they have received several Awards of Excellence from the Interior Design Institute of British Columbia.

The work of BattersbyHowat was also featured in the 2010 documentary *cArtographies*.

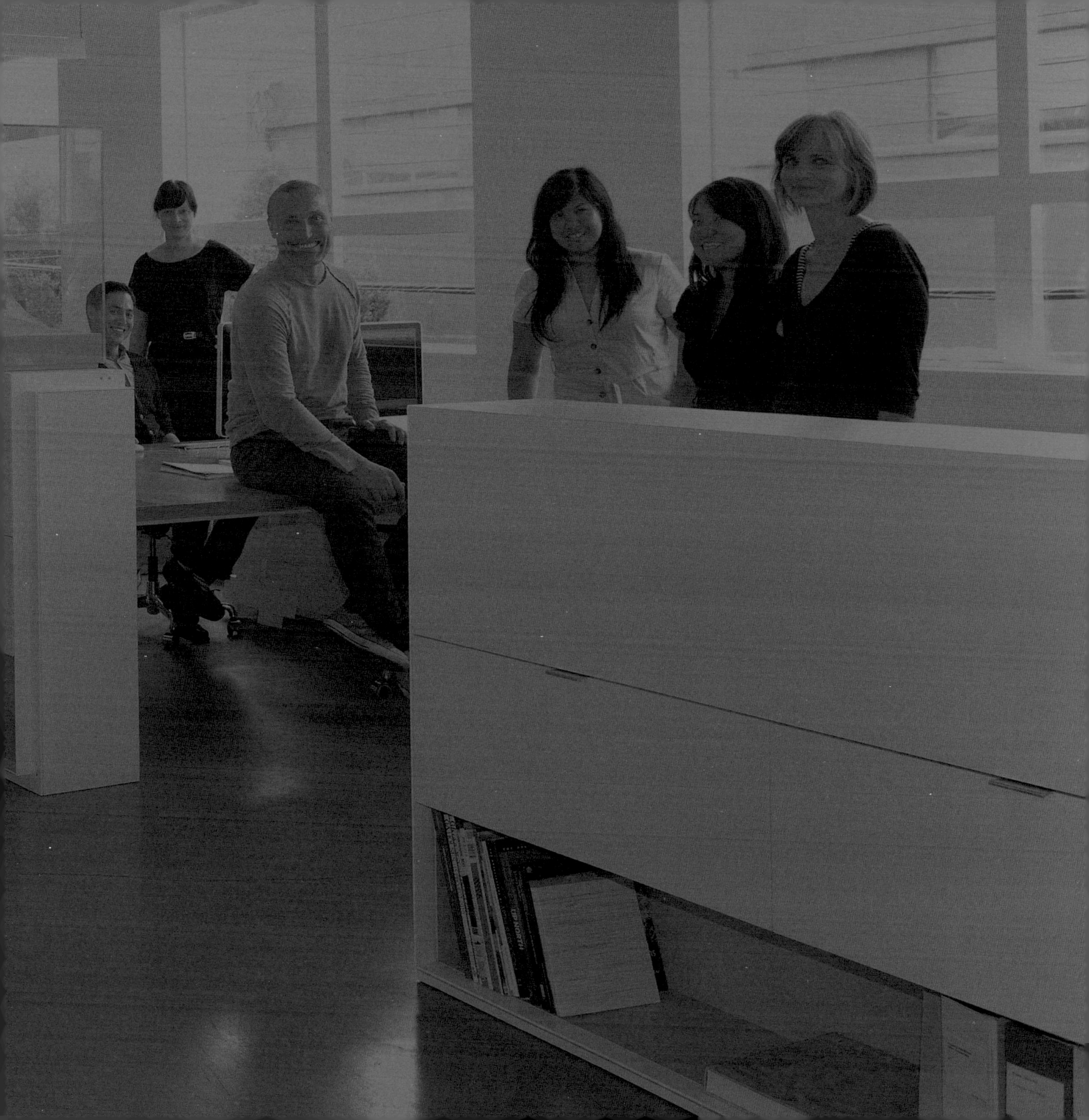

Timeline
2001-2011

2004, Gulf Island P 14

2004, North Bend P 22

2005, Bonetti P 28

2001

Project: **Midblock Residence**
Building Type: Residential, single-family
Location: Vancouver, BC, 2001

Project: **Corner House**
Building Type: Residential, single-family
Location: Vancouver, BC, 2001

Project: **East Georgia Duplex**
Building Type: Residential, multi-family
Location: Vancouver, BC, 2001

Awards: *Canadian Architect*, Award of Exellence, Gulf Island Residence, Gulf Islands, British Columbia

Exhibitions & Lectures: Weyerhauser Lecture Series, School of Architecture and Landscape Architecture, University of British Columbia, Vancouver

Selected Publications:
"Staehling Residence" *Canadian Architect*, Dec 2001

"Refined Renegades" *Azure*, Oct 2001

"Young Leaders: Architecture" *The Globe and Mail*, July 2000

2002

Project: **Living Space Showroom**
Building Type: Commercial interior
Location: Vancouver, BC
Status: Completed 2002

Selected Publications: "BattersbyHowat's Box Set" *Azure*, Dec 2002

2003

Exhibitions & Lectures:
West Coast Residential Symposium, Charles H. Scott Gallery, Vancouver

"Cabin + Camp" Symposium, School of Architecture and Landscape Architecture, University of British Columbia, Vancouver

"Architects in Collaboration" Architectural Institute of BC Annual Conference, Vancouver

Selected Publications:
"Mi casa, Su Casa" *Western Living*, Sep 2003

"House Turns Corner" *Arcade*, Spring 2003

2004

Project: **Gulf Island Residence**
Location: Gulf Islands, British Columbia
Site Area: 7400 ft^2 (1600 m^2)
Building Area: 2500 ft^2 (230 m^2)
Status: Completed 2004
Project team: David Battersby, Heather Howat
Consultants: Fast + Epp Structural Engineers Inc. (structural)

Project: **North Bend**
Building Type: Single-family residence
Location: North Bend, Washington, USA
Site Area: 3.5 acres (1.4 ha)
Building Area: 5000 ft^2 (465 m^2)
Status: On hold
Project team: David Battersby, Heather Howat, Tillie Kwan
Consultants: Fast + Epp Structural Engineers Inc. (structural)

Project: **East Pender Studio**
Building Type: Commercial, office building
Location: Vancouver, BC
Status: Completed 2004
Project team: David Battersby, Heather Howat

Awards: *Canadian Architect*, Award of exellence, Chamberland Residence

Selected Publications:
"North Bend Residence" *Canadian Architect*, Dec 2004

"Urbane Renewal" *Saturday Night*, Oct 2004

Wallpaper Design Directory

"The Simple Life" *Canadian House and Home*, May 2004

2005

Project: **Bonetti Residence**
Building Type: Single-family residence
Location: West Vancouver, British Columbia
Site Area: 22000 ft^2 (2000 m^2)
Building Area: 5500 ft^2 (510 m^2)
Status: Completed 2005
Project team: David Battersby, Heather Howat, Matthew McLeod
Consultants: Bevan-Pritchard Man (Structural)
Contractor: Canex Construction Ltd. with Powers Construction Ltd

2007, 2386 Cornwall   P 34

2007, Gambier 1   P 40

Project	**Ontario Residences**
Building Type	Residential, single-family
Location	Vancouver, BC, 2005

Project	**Nelson Avenue Residence**
Building Type	Residential, single-family
Location	West Vancouver, BC, 2005

Project	**Appleton Residence**
Building Type	Residential, single-family
Location	Saanich, BC, 2005

Project	**Prince Edward Residences**
Building Type	Residential, multi-family
Location	Vancouver, BC. 2005
Designers	David Battersby, Heather Howat
Architect	Hancock Bruckner Eng & Wright
Awards	2005 *Western Living's* Best in the West, Award for large house, Bonetti Residence
Exhibitions & Lectures	Substance over Spectacle" Exhibition Morris and Helen Belkin Gallery, Vancouver
	"21 Contemporary Canadian Homes" Living Spaces Exhibition, Cambridge, Toronto, Halifax
	"Movers and Shapers" Exhibition Vancouver Home and Interior Design Show, Vancouver
Selected Publication	"Living on the Edge" *Western Living*, Oct 2005
	Substance over Spectacle: Contemporary Canadian Architecture Arsenal Pulp Press, 2005 *Living Spaces: 21 Contemporary* Exhibition catalog, 2005

Cabin, Cottage and Camp: New Designs on the Canadian Landscape
Christopher Macdonald & Jana Tyner
Blue Imprint, 2005

"A Grand Façade"
Canadian House and Home, May 2005

"The Wilder Side of Modern"
Metropolitan Home, May 2005

"Island Lookout"
Azure, May 2005

2006

Project	**1181 Davie**
Building Type	Commercial interior
Location	Vancouver, BC, 2006
Designers	David Battersby, Heather Howat
Architect	Hancock Bruckner Eng & Wright

Project	**Battersby Residence**
Building Type	Residential, single-family
Location	Revelstoke, BC, 2006
Awards	*Western Living's* Best in the West, Award for medium house, Appleton Residence
	Ron Thom Award for Early Achievement in Architecture, Canada Council for the Arts
Exhibitions & Lectures	"West Coast Residential" Exhibition Architecture and Design Museum of Los Angeles
Selected Publications	"House Density" *Surface, 9th Annual Avant Guardian*

Issue, Western Living Viewfinder,
Oct 2006
"Viewfinder"
Western Living, Oct 2006

"Wild Life"
USA Home & Living Trends, vol. 22

"A Club of One's Own"
Canadian Architect, Sep 2006

2007

Project	**Gambier 1**
Building Type	Vacation home
Location	Gambier Island, British Columbia
Site Area	21000 ft^2 (1980 m^2)
Building Area	2000 ft^2 (185 m^2)
Status	Completed 2007
Project Team	David Battersby, Heather Howat Josie Grant
Consultants	Bevan-Pritchard Man (Structural)
Contractor	Hart + Tipton Construction Ltd.

Project	**2386 Cornwall**
Building Type	Multi-family residential
Location	Kitsilano, Vancouver, British Columbia
Site Area	4350 ft^2 (400 m^2)
Building Area	7830 ft^2 (727 m^2)
Status	Completed 2007
Project Team	David Battersby, Heather Howat Matthew McLeod
Consultants	Bevan-Pritchard Man (Structural)
Contractor	Hart + Tipton Construction Ltd
Architect of Record	Hancock Bruckner Eng + Wright
Consultants	RKTG Associates (Structural), AC Mechanical Solutions (Mechanical + Electrical), JRS Engineering Ltd. (Envelope)
Contractor	Brandes Development Corporation Ltd.

2008, Tolmie P 52   2010, Whistler P 60   2011, Salt Spring Island P 66

Project	**Belmont Residence**	
Building Type	Residential, single-family	
Location	North Vancouver, BC, 2007	
Project	**Yaletown Yoga**	
Building Type	Commercial interior	
Location	Vancouver, BC 2007	
Designers	David Battersby, Heather Howat	
Architect	Bob Turner	
Project	**Aritzia Headquarters**	
Building Type	Interior, corporate headquarters	
Location	Vancouver, BC, 2007-2011	
Designers	David Battersby, Heather Howat	
Architect	Bob Turner	
Awards	Award of Excellence, 1181 Davie Street, Interior Designers Institute of British Columbia	
Selected Publications	"Rise and Shine", *Azure*, May 2008	
	"Fine Lines" *The Block*, vol 1, issue 4	
	"Modern Living", *H.O.M.E.*, May 20	
	Young Architects Americas West Coast Residential: The Modern and the Contemporary Exhibition Catalog	
	Sustainable Environments Contemporary Design in Detail Series Rockport Press, 2007 "Block Party" *Canadian Architect*, Aug 2007	

2008

Project	**Tolmie**
Building Type	Single-family residence
Location	Vancouver, British Columbia
Site Area	8700 ft² (810 m²)
Building Area	3200 ft² (300 m²)
Status	Completed 2008
Project Team	David Battersby, Heather Howat Matthew Mcleod
Consultants	Chiu Webster Engineering (Structural)
Contractor	Hart + Tipton Construction Ltd.
Awards	Award of Excellence, Aritzia Studios, Interior Designers Institute of British Columbia
Exhibitions & Lectures	Carleton University School of Architecture Lecture Series National Gallery of Canada, Ottawa
Selected Publications	*The Cedar Book 2008: Inspiration for the Use of Western Red Cedar*

2009

Project	**West 7th Residence**
Building Type	Residential, single-family
Location	Vancouver, BC, 2009
Project	**Oyster Island Retreat**
Building Type	Residential, family retreat compound
Location	Oyster Island, BC, 2009
Project	**Cypress Residence**
Building Type	Residential, single-family
Location	Vancouver, BC, 2009

Exhibitions & Lectures	"The Roadshow: Architectural Landscapes of Canada" Vancouver, Calgary, Winnipeg, Toronto, Cambridge, Ottawa, Montreal, Halifax
Selected Publications	"Blond on Blond" *Azure*, Jun 2009
	"Blockhaus Mit Fokus" ("Narrowing the Focus") *Häuser*, Apr 2009

2010

Project	**Whistler Residence**
Building Type	Single-family residence
Location	Whistler, British Columbia
Site Area	11300 ft² (1050 m²)
Building Area	5800 ft2 (540 m2)
Status	Completed 2010
Project Team	David Battersby, Heather Howat, Tillie Kwan
Consultants	Equilibrium Consulting (Structural), JRS Engineering Ltd. (Envelope)
Contractor	Brophy Services Ltd.
Project	**Cambridge Residence**
Building Type	Residential, single-family
Location	Burnaby, BC, 2010
Project	**The Keefer**
Building Type	Commercial interior
Location	Vancouver, BC, 2010
Designers	David Battersby, Heather Howat
Architect	Gair Williamson
Project	**Sooke Residence**
Building Type	Residential, single-family
Location	Sooke, BC, 2010

2011, Gambier 2   P 72

2011, Fairmile   P 80

Exhibitions & Lectures	"Banff Session 2010" Alberta Association of Architects Banff
Selected Publications	"Escape to the Rock" *Dwell*, Nov 2010 "Casa per vacanze a Gambier Island, Vancouver, British Columbia" ("Vacation Home on Gambier Island") *L'Insdustria Delle Construzioni 421: Architettura Canadese*, Mar 2010 "A Family Home" *Westcoast Homes & Design*, Mar 2010 "Sun 1" *A Guidebook to Contemporary Architecture in Vancouver* Douglas & McIntyre, 2010

2011

Project	**Thompson Crescent Residence**
Building Type	Residential, single-family
Location	West Vancouver, BC, 2011

Project	**Salt Spring Island Residence**
Building Type	Vacation home
Location	Salt Spring Island, British Columbia
Site Area	5.0 acres (2.0 ha)
Building Area	3000 ft^2 (275 m^2)
Status	Completed 2011
Project Team	David Battersby, Heather Howat, Cindy Lee
Consultants	Bevan-Pritchard Man (Structural)
Contractor	Delburn Developments Inc.

Project	**Merritt Residence**
Building Type	Residential, single-family
Location	Vancouver, BC, 2011

Project	**Gambier 2**
Building Type	Single-family residence
Location	Gambier Island, British Columbia
Site Area	43 acres (17 ha)
Building Area	3500 ft^2 (325 m^2)
Status	Completed 2011
Project Team	David Battersby, Heather Howat, Tillie Kwan, Cindy Lee
Consultants	Bevan-Pritchard Man (Structural)
Contractor	Dennis Parolin and Highliner Construction Ltd.

Project	**Eppich House Renovation**
Building Type	Interior
Location	Vancouver, BC, 2011
Designers	BattersbyHowat
Architect	Arthur Erickson

Project	**Fairmile**
Building Type	Single-family residence
Location	West Vancouver, British Columbia
Site Area	14800 ft^2 (1375 m^2)
Building Area	4600 ft^2 (425 m^2)
Status	Construction documentation
Project Team	David Battersby, Heather Howat, Mary Cuk
Consultants	Ennova Structural Engineers Inc. (Structural), JRS Engineering Ltd. (Envelope)

Awards	Design Exchange Awards, Silver, Interior Design – Residential, Cypress Residence, Vancouver Designer of the Year, Architecture and Interior Design, *Western Living Magazine*

Exhibitions & Lectures	"Prototypes" Design exhibition presented by Burnkit Vancouver
Selected Publications	"Inside & Out" *Western Living*, Sep 2011 "Rustique confortable" *Architecture Bois,* Jul 2011 "Canadian Homes Staying by Nature" *I'm Home,* May 2011

Contributors

Christopher Macdonald is Professor of Architecture in the School of Architecture and Landscape Architecture at the University of British Columbia. A graduate of the University of Manitoba and the Architectural Association, he was a founding partner of Macdonald and Salter in London. Their work was published internationally and exhibited at the Storefront for Art & Architecture in New York and other notable venues.

Professor Macdonald was co-curator of Sweaterlodge, Canada's contribution to the 2006 Venice Biennale in Architecture. A Fellow of the RAIC, he is the author of *A Guide to Contemporary Architecture in Vancouver* published by Douglas & McIntyre in 2010.

Christine Macy is Dean of the School of Architecture at Dalhousie University. A graduate of UC Berkeley and MIT she worked in practice in New York and San Francisco before taking up a teaching appointment in Canada. Together with Sarah Bonnemaison she founded FILUM in 1990, a studio that specializes in the design of lightweight structures and public spaces in architecture.

Dean Macy teaches design and modern architectural history and theory. She is also the author of numerous books on architecture. A co-author of *Architecture and Nature* that was published by Routledge in 2004, her most recent book, which focused on the design and construction of dams, was published by W.W.Norton & Company in 2010.

Brian Carter, a registered architect in the UK, is Professor of Architecture at the University at Buffalo, The State University of New York where he also served as Dean from 2003-2011. A graduate of Nottingham School of Architecture and the University of Toronto, he worked in practice with Arup in London prior to taking up an academic appointment in North America.

The designer of several award-winning buildings he also writes about architecture. His work has been published in numerous international journals including *Casabella*, *Detail*, *AD*, and *The Architectural Review*. Professor Carter is the author of several books on architecture including *Johnson Wax Administration Building & Research Tower* which was published by Phaidon Press.

Acknowledgements

To: all of our clients (now friends) who have had faith in our designs and contributed so much to our process and their individual projects.

All the contractors and subcontractors who have helped realize our visions over the years and taught us so much along the way.

The many inspiring local and international architects that have fed our imaginations.

The many writers and photographers we've worked with to promote and document the work.

All of our staff throughout the years that have been so dedicated to open communication and high design standards and putting up with a formerly married couple who still bicker like one. We are lucky to have had so many talented and genuine individuals close to us.

Ben, Mona, and Matt for keeping this book on track every step of the way.

Burnkit for stepping into the fray.

Chris for being an early supporter and for his generous words in this book.

Christine for genuinely inspiring and challenging us as students.

Brian for suggesting that this book be initiated and then not losing patience as it slowly came into fruition. He would like to acknowledge support for his work on this publication from the Canadian-American Studies Committee at the University at Buffalo, The State University of New York and the Government of Canada and the help of Dr. L. Oak.

Tuns Press and Dalhousie University for the opportunity.

We acknowledge the support of the Canada Council for the Arts, which last year invested $154 million to bring the arts to Canadians throughout the country.

Nous remercions le Conseil des Arts du Canada de son soutien. L'an dernier, le Conseil a investi 154 millions de dollars pour mettre de l'art dans la vie des Canadiennes et des Canadiens de tout le pays.

Conseil des arts du Canada   Canada Council for the Arts

Photography Credits

Tom Arban: p.14, 17, 19, 20, 21

BattersbyHowat: p.2-3, 6, 12-13, 31 (left), 32, 33, 49, 63 (bottom), 76

Michael Boland: p.37, 39 (right)

Sama J. Canzian: p.60, 63 (top), 64, 65, 66, 69, 70-71, 72, 75, 77, 78, 79

Josh Dunford: 86-87, 92, 94-95, inside front and back cover

Ivan Hunter: p.34, 39 (top, bottom), 40, 45, 46 (left), 47, 48, 52, 56-57, 58, 59

Tomas Machnikowski (model): p.22, 25, 80, 82-83

Matthew Millman: p.43, 50, 51

Martin Tessler: p.28, 31 (right)

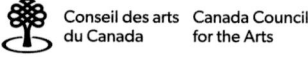

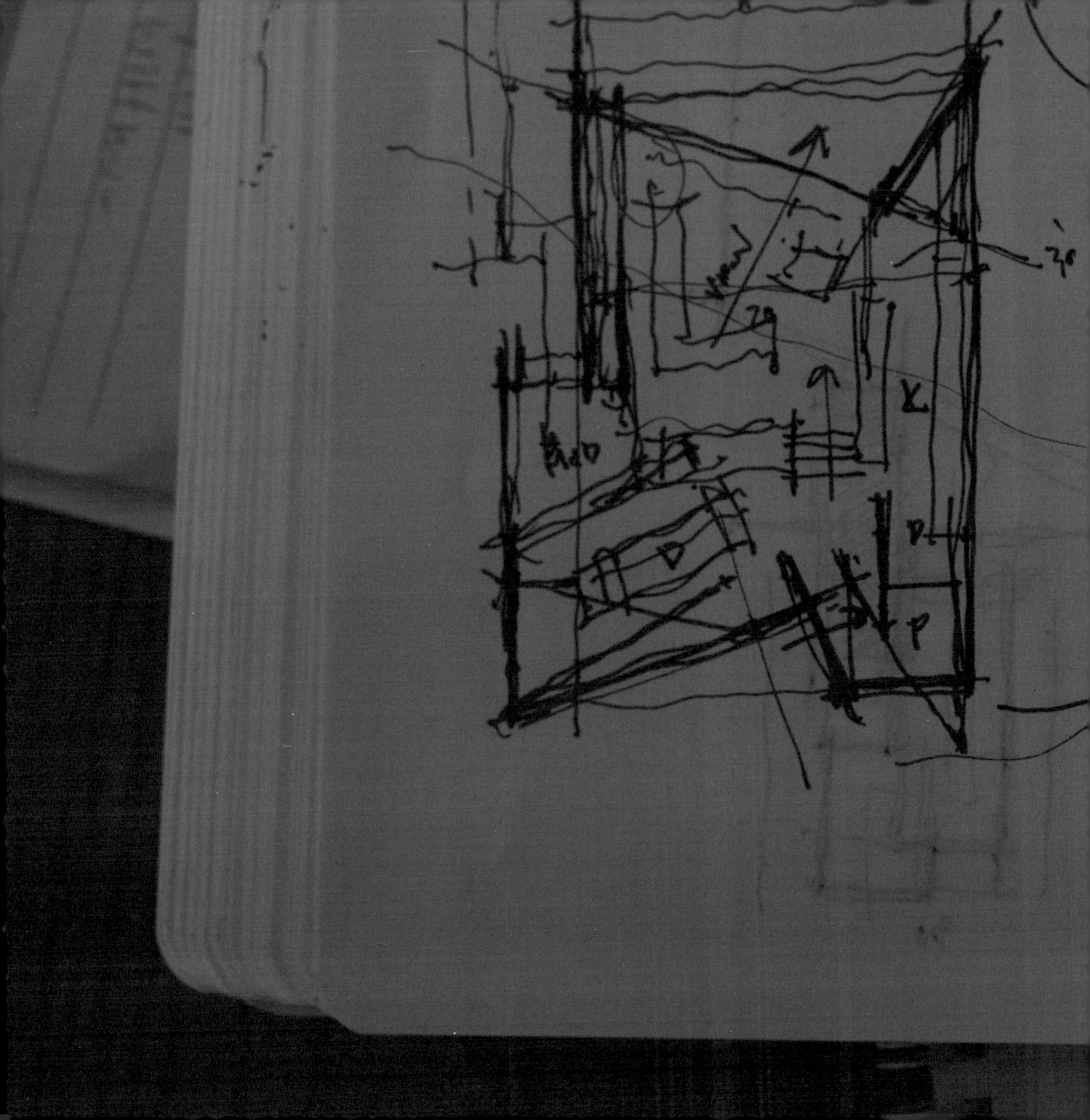

- POOL IN FRONT YARD NO SIDE YARD
  SET BACK